# ABOVE STAIRS

# ABOVE STAIRS

## Social Life in Upper-Class Victoria 1843–1918

VALERIE GREEN

TouchWood
Editions

TouchWood Editions
www.touchwoodeditions.com

LIBRARY AND ARCHIVES CANADA CATALOGUING IN PUBLICATION
Green, Valerie, 1940–
Above stairs : social life in upper-class
Victoria, 1843–1918 / Valerie Green.

Includes bibliographical references and index.
Issued also in electronic formats.
ISBN 978-1-926971-62-9

1. Upper class families—British Columbia—Victoria—Biography.
2. Upper class—British Columbia—Victoria—Social life and customs.
3. Victoria (BC)—Social life and customs. 4. Victoria (BC)—History. I. Title.

FC3846.394.G74 2011          971.1'28          C2011-904155-3

Editor: Marlyn Horsdal
Proofreader: Sarah Weber
Design: Pete Kohut
Front cover image: Image F-02196 courtesy of Royal BC Museum, BC Archives
Back cover image: Cynthia Sellers, stock.xchng

BRITISH COLUMBIA ARTS COUNCIL    Canada Council for the Arts    Conseil des Arts du Canada    Canadian Heritage    Patrimoine canadien

We gratefully acknowledge the financial support for our publishing activities
from the Government of Canada through the Canada Book Fund, Canada
Council for the Arts, and the province of British Columbia through the
British Columbia Arts Council and the Book Publishing Tax Credit.

MIX
Paper from
responsible sources
FSC® C016245

The interior pages of this book have been printed on 100% post-consumer
recycled paper, processed chlorine free, and printed with vegetable-based inks.

1  2  3  4  5  15  14  13  12  11

PRINTED IN CANADA

This book is dedicated to the pioneering spirit of our ancestors, whether they be upper, middle or lower class. We are indebted to them all.

And, in particular, to my own family of ancestors of

Stofers
Dibbens
Coulsons
Barbers
Greens
MacDonalds and
Gunns

many of whom were in a class all their own.

Sir James Douglas.
IMAGE A-01229 COURTESY OF ROYAL BC MUSEUM, BC ARCHIVES

The Hudson's Bay Company having formed an establishment on the southern point of Vancouver's Island, which they are annually enlarging, are anxious to know whether they will be confirmed in the possession of such lands, as they may find it expedient to add to those which they already possess.

—Sir John Pelly, Governor of the HBC to Earl Grey, Britain's Colonial Secretary, 7th September, 1846 [Great Britain, Parliament, House of Commons, Sessional Papers, 1846-48, No. 619, p. 3]

Lady Amelia Douglas.

# CONTENTS

ഗ ഗ ഗ

The establishment and subsequent growth of Victoria, British Columbia, from fort to capital city and beyond, is a fascinating story, and one of the most interesting aspects of that story is the social life enjoyed by the people who formed an upper-class network and came to think of themselves as the aristocracy of a new land.

In nineteenth-century England, those who were employed as servants spent most of their working days in the basements and cellars of the grand mansions owned by the wealthy elite. The term "below stairs" was coined to describe them. Conversely, those who owned the large homes were said to be living "above stairs." These terms were popularized by a BBC-TV series produced by Masterpiece Theatre, "Upstairs, Downstairs," which originally ran from 1971 to 1975. Even people who left Victorian England for foreign shores, such as Vancouver Island, perpetuated this class division; this book describes those who came to Victoria and lived, loved, and died above stairs.

I have chosen to describe eight specific pioneer families: the Douglases, the Skinners, the Pembertons, the Creases, the O'Reillys, the Trutches, the Rithets, and the Barnards. These families were selected merely as examples. Others, such as the Dunsmuirs, the Todds, the Kers, and the Spencers (to name but a few), were of equal importance and could well have been included had space permitted.

The eight chosen, however, were important because of their contributions to society at various stages in the seventy-five years of Victoria's history about which I have written. In essence, they represent the structure and gradual development of the province of British Columbia.

The Douglases were the element needed to govern the colony with stringent rules in the beginning; the Skinners were one of the families that farmed the land and became part of the rural gentry; the Pembertons surveyed the wilderness and carved out the beginnings of a city; the Creases upheld the laws of the land; the O'Reillys were one of the first families to set higher social standards; the Trutches were a major part of the transition from royal governors to lieutenant-governors, as well as excellent examples of the inadvertent snobbery of the times; the Rithets introduced the commercial element of entrepreneurship to the social scene; and the Barnards were leaders in a world that was quickly changing, with war clouds on the horizon. The Barnards' time at Government House heralded the end of the old order and the beginning of a new era with different social standards.

In reality, however, this elite circle of settlers was merely one part of the establishment on Vancouver Island. They were simply the ones with the right connections, leadership skills a little above the rest, and a definite belief in their own superiority.

Their place in high society came about initially as a result of a close association with the Hudson's Bay Company, sometimes in the form of a letter of introduction. As the years went by, it was also important to be connected socially to the Royal Navy. Later still, political links became significant.

They did not inherit their distinguished status by virtue of land ownership, family title, or blue blood, as might have been the case in the old world. It is interesting, therefore, to discover how and why these people came to form the ruling hierarchy in the new colony.

My intention throughout has been to portray the aristocratic lifestyle of these families as they went about their daily business: dining together, worshipping together, entertaining one another, and holding splendidly extravagant weddings and funerals. While the men discussed the politics of the day and made decisions on the future policy of the province, the women held at-homes and gossiped about the affairs around them as they played hostess with grace and charm.

Their homes were elegantly built, modelled along the lines of all that was finest in the old world. Their children played together and went to the best schools back east or in Europe, and, on occasion, their families intermarried.

What follows is a glimpse of life "above stairs" in those resplendent days of long ago, when snobbery was rife, and when wealth, education, the right connections, and an added touch of charm dictated one's place in high society.

# In the Institutions of the Old

The object of every sound system of colonization should be, not to re-organize Society on a new basis, which is simply absurd, but to transfer to the new country whatever is most valuable and most approved in the institutions of the old, so that society may, as far as possible, consist of the same classes, united together by the same ties and having the same relative duties to perform in one country as in the other.

—Barclay to Douglas, December 1849: Quoted from
*Land Policy of the Colony of Vancouver Island, 1849–1866*

In order to set the scene, it is neces-sary to emphasize that it was the twenty years between 1840 and 1860 that opened up the west. During that time, the North American population grew and expanded in a westerly direction at a rapid rate. It was an exciting time, full of promise and hope, and countless adventurous men and women wanted to be a part of it. The challenge of the unknown spurred many a courageous heart to leave behind all that was familiar and start afresh in some far-flung outpost of civilization.

So it was with those who settled in Victoria, British Columbia's capital. They left the land of their birth for various reasons, but they arrived in the new world with the same burning desire to build an ideal settlement. What they did not realize was that although they were rebuilding their lives in another place geographically, their building tools were the same as they had always been—the long-established traditions, values, customs, and beliefs they held. They were, in fact, merely creating another small part of the empire in their adopted land.

Many people consider the gold rush of 1858 to be the beginning of Victoria's settlement, but it began long before that. Victoria, both socially and economically, grew at the hand of the Hudson's Bay Company, that gallant "Company of Adventurers of England Trading into Hudson's Bay," founded in England in 1670.

By the early part of the nineteenth century, the company had expanded across the North American continent, and in 1820, Fort Vancouver on the Columbia River became its western headquarters. While it continued to trade very profitably in furs, negotiations were ongoing concerning the location of the boundary between British and American territory. When it became obvious that the forty-ninth parallel would be the point of demarcation, rather than the Columbia River, the company decided to look for new headquarters.

The southerly tip of Vancouver Island was considered to be the ideal location. In all probability, it would remain under British rule. A young fur trader with the company, James Douglas, was assigned to explore the area. Douglas set about this formidable task in 1842. In the spring of 1843 he finally found what he considered to be the perfect site, and the construction of Fort Victoria began immediately.

Even the company men, however, cannot truly be considered the original establishment of Victoria. The First Nations played an important role as the first inhabitants and traders in the area. According to G.P.V. & Helen B. Akrigg's *British Columbia Chronicle (1778–1846)*, Native lore, memory, and legend extend back only two hundred years before the coming of the white man in 1778, but they had lived on the land now known as British Columbia for perhaps thousands of years before that.

By the middle of the nineteenth century, Victoria had become the central point for much trading activity between the local peoples and the white man. Salmon, potatoes, and fur were traded for blankets and ammunition.

In January 1849, six years after the establishment of Fort Victoria, the British government granted formal control of Vancouver Island to the HBC in exchange for seven shillings a year for the next ten years. The company was also strongly encouraged to establish a British settlement within five years.

Colonial Secretary Earl Grey had always come down in favour of British immigration and colonization on Vancouver Island. The HBC governor, Sir John Pelly, agreed wholeheartedly. He had expressed as much in many of his letters. In one, for example, he stated,

> the colonization of Vancouver's Island [is] an object of great importance; I shall, at present, merely submit to Earl Grey's consideration whether that object, embracing as I trust it will, the conversion to Christianity and civilization of the native population, might not be most readily and effectually accomplished through the instrumentality of the Hudson's Bay Company."[1]

It was generally agreed that the best form of colonization was to "recreate on Vancouver Island the social structure of England, a stalwart squirearchy with the working class properly relegated to an inferior station."[2] This rather high-handed, snobbish attitude of the company gives a clear picture of what was expected of Victoria's early settlement.

There was, according to the company, a need for British gentlemen who were well placed in life and would have the wherewithal to purchase large acreages of land for one pound per acre. They would then be expected to employ one labourer for every twenty acres. It was not a popular concept and apparently did not work well for, by December 1854, a census compiled by James Douglas showed there were still only two hundred and thirty-two settlers in Victoria, and even by 1858 the population had reached barely three hundred.

It can be assumed from this scenario that the company did not keep its end of the bargain. It made no overt attempts to foster colonization and tended, for its own purposes, to concentrate on fur trading. However, in fairness, it should also be said that in order to strengthen the economy, it did give some support to other industries such as coal-mining and fishing.

More importantly, although the company still discouraged colonists from settling within a twenty-mile radius of Fort Victoria (the land known as the fur trade reserve), it did make an attempt at bringing in men who would establish Victoria as an agricultural centre.

Captain Walter Colquhoun Grant was an example of the kind of colonist the company wanted. He hailed from Scotland and, having recently lost all his money through gambling, had resigned his commission there with the 2nd Dragoons, the Scots Greys, and was more than ready for adventure. With the promise of work as a surveyor with the company, in addition to what he would make as a gentleman farmer, he felt confident of his success. He was young and full of hope. A large man standing well over six feet, he was also blessed with a certain undeniable charm. In fact, Dr. James Helmcken described him in his *Reminiscences* as "a splendid fellow and every inch a gentleman."[3] He was, however, sadly lacking in experience and common sense.

Grant's uncle had given him money for his passage to the new world, as well as supplying funds for the purchase of land on Vancouver Island. Passage for eight men to be hired as Grant's labourers had also been paid by his uncle. These men set sail in November 1848 aboard the company's ship, the *Harpooner*. In June 1849 they arrived at Fort Victoria and waited anxiously for their employer. Captain Grant did not appear until August. He had apparently taken the Panama railway route to reach Victoria, supposedly to avoid the long voyage around Cape Horn, but he had spent all his money by the time he reached San Francisco.

There it had been necessary for an HBC agent to advance him money for his passage to Victoria. Along the way, Grant had mislaid his surveying tools, and upon his arrival in Victoria, he supposedly shot a cow, mistaking it for a buffalo. It was not the most auspicious of beginnings for Victoria's first settler.

Captain Grant was offered land twenty-five miles from Fort Victoria in what is today the Sooke area. He cleared land for his wilderness home, known as Mullachard, and began planting and cultivating the soil. Cattle grazed on the remainder of his property and he even built a sawmill. His intention was to establish a small Scottish colony in the wilderness, but lack of expertise, coupled with the discontent of his men, doomed his endeavours to failure. With precious little financial success, he was eventually forced to discharge the men.

He then took up Douglas's offer of some surveying work, but again his abilities, once put to the test, were sadly lacking. In the face of so many problems, and probably suffering loneliness in the isolation of his property, he decided to take a trip to the Sandwich Islands (Hawaii) for a few months to forget his problems. He returned in February 1851, bringing with him some broom seeds given to him by the British consul. These he planted near his Sooke home. Soon the broom had spread over the entire southern coast of the island, and remains today as the only reminder of Victoria's first settler.

Grant did not stay long in the colony. During the months before he departed for good, he frequently passed his time at the fort in the company of other Hudson's Bay men who enjoyed drinking as much as he did. The frequent downing of whisky in jovial company was the only thing that made his life bearable. Totally unsuited to colonial life, he eventually sold his Sooke property to Thomas Muir and promptly left for Oregon in search of gold, an endeavour that also proved fruitless. In 1853, a report of his activities stated that Grant had not a cent to his name, and he was off to Mexico to try his luck there.

Returning to England, Grant joined his old regiment at the time of the Crimean War. In January 1857, before the Royal Geographical Society in London, he read his paper, "Description of Vancouver Island," for which he was greatly praised and commended. This, and a subsequent paper submitted to the society in December 1859, were perhaps Grant's greatest contributions to colonization and appear to somewhat redeem his character from a historical perspective. He later served with distinction in his regiment in India and died there from dysentery in August 1861.

Meanwhile, Douglas had other problems to deal with. Many of the men at the fort were leaving, lured by news from the California goldfields, and the labour shortage forced him to hire Native people. Employing the local people and the Kanakas (Native people originally from Hawaii) to work the farms or man the ships meant that it was essential to maintain good relations between colonists and Native people. Also, he was being pressured by the Colonial Office in London to ensure that the colonists would be protected in the event of any future trouble over land claims. To this end, on April 29, 1850, Douglas negotiated the first of thirteen treaties at Fort Victoria. All the treaties clearly identified the land that was to be surrendered to the HBC, as well as the exact payment to be made.

Other settlers did slowly begin to arrive at Fort Victoria during the 1850s, following Captain Grant's departure. Two early arrivals were the Reverend Robert Staines and his wife, Emma, who came aboard the HBC barque *Columbia* to teach school in the colony.

In March 1850, the *Norman Morison* arrived in Esquimalt Harbour with over eighty immigrants, including one well-trained doctor from London, John Sebastian Helmcken. As the fort's first doctor, he was to become famous and very well loved by many generations of Victorians.

More settlers continued to trickle in. They came on other immigrant vessels such as the *Tory*. Many settlers—the Langfords, the McKenzies, and the Skinners among them—came as employees of the Puget Sound Agricultural Company (a subsidiary of the HBC).

Nevertheless, population growth was slow and Victoria remained little more than a rural village. Then, in the spring of 1858, this state of affairs changed overnight when the first of British Columbia's gold rushes took place on the Fraser River. The subsequent influx of immigrants, starting with the arrival of the *Commodore* in April of that year, was unprecedented. With a white population of little over three hundred at first, Victoria became a town of three thousand by year's end. This figure sometimes rose as high as six thousand if transients were included. It was an interesting, highly colourful population composed of many races and cultures, which brought with it a boosted economy but also numerous problems for Victoria.

A few years earlier, following Captain Grant's short and unproductive career, Douglas had secured the skills of a far more proficient surveyor. Joseph Despard Pemberton was a competent and experienced man. He arrived in Victoria in June 1851 and immediately set about resurveying the fur trade reserve and laying out a plan for a town adjacent to the fort. His plan is worthy of praise, for it stood the test of time through Victoria's two gold rushes and its incorporation as a city in 1862.

The plan adhered to the accepted principles of colonization at that time. These were that the "most valuable and most approved," as Barclay had put it, individuals in British society would be encouraged to settle in Victoria. It was apparent that the old class system, so ingrained in Britain, would continue in the new colony.

Pemberton's aim was to concentrate settlement within the town itself while encouraging farming in the surrounding areas. He was sure that up to that point, colonization had failed mainly because of Vancouver Island's distance from Great Britain. A five-month-long sea voyage and an expensive overland route via the Panama Canal did not make the most attractive of prospects. In addition, the colonist was faced with the lure of California's gold regions so near. Many had even stopped off in San Francisco en route to Victoria, deciding to abandon their original plans and stay on in California. Land was expensive on Vancouver Island, compared with its price in Oregon, and the level of wages was far from satisfactory.

Pemberton laid out his clear and concise plan to help improve conditions and override these setbacks. The colonist, he believed, needed to be induced into coming to Vancouver Island. He needed to be sufficiently attracted by the island's prospects to risk his all by crossing an ocean into the unknown.

The price of land at one pound an acre, with grants of no less than twenty acres, Pemberton believed to be the first incentive. Passage at reasonable rates was also held out as a carrot to attract the colonist. And, although any minerals discovered on the land would automatically belong to the HBC, the owner would be allowed to work for his own benefit any coal mine that might be on his land, on payment of royalty of half a crown per ton. Fishing rights were given to the colonist, and an added attraction was the fact that all ports and harbours were open and free.

Despite all this, real success in colonization did not come about until after the first gold rush of 1858. It can, therefore, be surmised that one of the foremost reasons why any man decided to uproot himself and his family in order to travel to the other side of the world was simply that he had developed a bad case of gold fever.

The British government had seen the need to colonize Vancouver Island as protection against the threat of further American infiltration. What happened in 1858 and again in 1862, however, was certainly not what the government had envisioned, for among the numerous nationalities arriving in Victoria were many Americans.

Nonetheless, the colonists with British backgrounds gradually grew in number until Victoria's original establishment became so strongly entrenched in society that even the new cosmopolitan atmosphere developing alongside it could not destroy it. In the final analysis, it would seem that Pemberton's town plan and his ideas for colonization were indeed successful and would have continued to be successful, albeit more slowly, even had there not been a gold rush.

Other ethnic groups brought with them new and diverse religions, as well as their culture and customs. Victoria's society became a mixture of many things, but one aspect did not change. A strong division of class was still evident: the upper echelon of the population continued to set the tone and pace of life in those early years.

These people were an elite and powerful group of settlers who became the aristocracy of Victoria. Their backgrounds varied, and in many cases those backgrounds were quite unremarkable. Once they were established in their chosen new life, however, their uniqueness, coupled with a broad visionary awareness of what was required to make that new life successful, enabled them to turn those pasts into phenomenal futures. Names such as Douglas, Skinner, and Pemberton were the foundation of that new world. In due course, other names such as Crease, O'Reilly, Rithet, Trutch, and Barnard, joined the group. This new breed of colonist was the beginning of a dynasty.

As the stories of these families unfold, the social life they enjoyed will be explored and examined. Their new world was still very young and vulnerable, but the colony's upper-class citizens intended to establish a society fashioned according to the institutions of the old world they had forsaken in favour of greener pastures in Victoria.

Consequently, without realizing it, they created instead a unique community halfway between British traditionalism and North American brashness.

# THE FAMILIES

## The Douglas Family

Amelia Douglas surrounded by her family.
IMAGE G-03584 COURTESY OF ROYAL BC MUSEUM, BC ARCHIVES

No history of the province can be written without Sir James Douglas forming the central figure around which will cluster the stirring events that have marked the advance of the province from a fur-hunting preserve for nomadic tribes to a progressive country of civilized beings, under the protection of the British Flag and enjoying a stable and settled form of government.

—*Victoria Colonist*, August 4, 1877

On August 14, 1863, James Douglas, governor of British Columbia, was elevated to the position of Knight Commander of the Most Honourable Order of the Bath. Thereafter he was to be known as Sir James Douglas.

An official ceremony took place at the old legislative buildings in Victoria, known as the Birdcages. This was followed by a private dinner hosted by Matthew Begbie, judge of the colony of British Columbia. It was a glittering affair with good food, fine wine, and numerous congratulatory speeches that went on far into the night. Judge Begbie, being a bachelor, had asked Sir James's wife, Amelia, to act as hostess.

A shy, retiring woman, Amelia (Connolly) Douglas had long served in her husband's shadow. It was the way she preferred it; she did not by choice seek the limelight. She had spent too many years trying to overcome the prejudices of a snobbish society that considered her mixed blood to be inferior. This night, however, was different. At last the spotlight was focused on Amelia, and for her the occasion would prove to be a personal triumph.

After dinner, Judge Begbie pinned the order of knighthood on Sir James Douglas's coat and placed the crimson collar and pendant around his neck. Then, raising his glass in Amelia's direction, he bowed with an elegant flourish and the words:

To our esteemed hostess, Lady Douglas, the wife of the Governor of British Columbia, and the first lady in the land.

Amelia Douglas had arrived. She was now part of the upper-class establishment of Victoria.

# CHAPTER ONE

# Spanish Brown with an Abundance of Whitewash

If it is true that the history of Victoria's upper-class social life begins with the Douglas family, then this narrative must start many miles away in Demerara, British Guiana (now Guyana). It was there that a son was born in 1803 to a Creole woman. The child's father was a prosperous Scottish merchant named John Douglas who held interests in South American sugar plantations.

Douglas did not marry his Creole mistress, despite having two sons and a daughter by her. He did, however, take full responsibility for those children, arranging for their later education in Lanark, Scotland. Then, in 1809, he decided to marry Jessie Hamilton of Glasgow and had three more daughters by her.

The child born in Demerara in 1803 was James Douglas, who would establish Fort Victoria and, during his lifetime, become known as "The Father of British Columbia." James Douglas's actual date of birth has frequently been the subject of contention. He himself recorded it as June 5, but his descendants believed it was August 15, and this date is carved on his monument in Ross Bay Cemetery in Victoria.

Having completed his education in Scotland by the age of fifteen, James Douglas sought his father's permission to travel to North America and pursue a career in the fur trade with the North West Company. His older brother, Alexander, had already taught him something of the trade and so, in May 1819, he set sail from Liverpool, England, aboard the *Matthew*.

He received his first instructions in Montreal. He was assigned to Fort William and travelled there by canoe. Those first years in the unexplored continent were full of adventures that were all eagerly embraced by the young man. Douglas was tall and very strong, and he always cut a striking figure. He also gained a reputation of being somewhat hotheaded and was frequently reprimanded by his superiors. One incident in 1820, when he was transferred to Île-à-la-Crosse, resulted in his fighting a duel with an employee of the rival Hudson's Bay Company. Fortunately, no blood was spilled.

Later, when the HBC amalgamated with the NWC and merged all their operations, Douglas was faced with a career decision—either to leave the fur trade completely or transfer his loyalties to the new company. He chose the latter.

In 1825 at twenty-two, James Douglas crossed the Rocky Mountains and set foot for the first time in New Caledonia (now British Columbia). In November he arrived at McLeod Lake where John Tod was the officer in charge.

He was then posted to Fort St. James to serve under Chief Factor William Connolly, the man who would become his father-in-law. In April 1828, Douglas entered a form of marriage, legal but known at that time as "the custom of the country," with Connolly's sixteen-year-old daughter, Amelia. Connolly himself officiated at the ceremony.

In many ways James's and Amelia's backgrounds were similar, for she was born of a union between Connolly and a Cree woman named Miyo Nipiy. Although Amelia's father lived with Miyo Nipiy for nearly thirty years, also in a custom-of-the-country marriage, he never legally married her and eventually left her to marry Julia Woolrich, a white woman.

For most of her life, Amelia was very conscious of her mixed-race background. Nevertheless, she agreed to enter into a similar marriage arrangement with James Douglas and had already borne him six children before they were more formally married in February 1837. This ceremony, performed by the Reverend Herbert Beaver, firmly cemented their already happy union. It is ironic that James and Amelia Douglas, who later became the central figures in Victoria's early social life and the arbiters of all moral convention, both came from multiracial backgrounds.

During the early years of their life together, Douglas spent many hours reading and improving his knowledge of world conditions so that he could clearly and concisely write down his own observations of pioneer life. It is believed that forty-five volumes of British classics, as well as *A History of England*, a French dictionary, and numerous other textbooks, accompanied him when he first came to BC, and he read them numerous times through the years.

William Connolly frequently warned Douglas about his short temper and advised him that co-operation and friendship with the local people were essential if the fur trade were to survive. This advice was put to the test on one occasion when Douglas was left in charge of the fort in Connolly's absence. Chief Kwah of the Carrier Nation forced entry into the fort by flashing a dagger at Douglas, who immediately lunged for his musket. Douglas was not quite quick enough; three of Kwah's warriors swiftly pinned him to the ground and tied him with a rope. The chief then told Douglas he had come to avenge the earlier killing of one of his own men, Zulth-Nolly, by Douglas and some HBC men.

Douglas, "damning and swearing and calling them big rascals," eventually quieted down, remembered Connolly's advice, and calmly explained why it had been necessary to kill Zulth-Nolly.[4] Five years earlier he had murdered some company men at Fort George, leaving their bodies to the village dogs. His killing had, therefore, been an act of justice by the company men, explained Douglas.

Chief Kwah was a man of honour. He admired Douglas's calm approach to the tense situation. In addition, Amelia and some other women at the fort began to throw down blankets, tobacco, and clothing for the warriors as a trade offering in exchange for Amelia's husband's life. The chief decided not only to spare Douglas's life but also to accept the goods as payment for the insult to his village, and an unpleasant situation was averted.

James and Amelia had many more such adventures through the years. Then, in 1840, after twenty-one years of service to the company, Douglas was promoted to chief factor and began concentrating his time and effort on surveying the Pacific coast, eventually establishing Fort Victoria.

At the fort, James Douglas insisted upon a certain standard of social behaviour from his men. He strongly believed in good citizenship and gentlemanly conduct in all things. His standards were high and he implemented all that he himself had learned. Control of one's temper at all times was paramount, as was courtesy to one's fellow man and strict obedience to the company. These standards, laid down by Douglas, were to become the foundation upon which Victoria's early social life was based.

The fort, which became the obvious centre of all social activity, was a quadrangle, "about one hundred yards long and wide, with bastions at two corners containing cannon."[5] The outer stockade was built of fifteen-foot cedar posts, brought in by the Native people from Cedar Hill (now Mount Douglas), and inside it there were twelve one-and-a-half-storey buildings. These included storage buildings, an Indian trading shop, and a large general trading store.

The Douglas family lived in quarters at the mess-room, and another family, the Finlaysons, occupied what was known as the counting house. The belfry bell, in the middle of the yard, tolled regularly for meals, deaths, weddings, church services, fires, and, on occasion, to warn of approaching danger.

According to Dr. Helmcken, the fort doctor and later son-in-law of James Douglas, the prevailing colour of paint used throughout the fort was "Spanish brown" and "whitewash was abundant."[6]

By far the most interesting section of Fort Victoria was Bachelors' Hall, a large portion of the building housing a common room in its centre with four rooms leading off it (two on each side). Three of these rooms were occupied by Dr. Helmcken, J.W. McKay, and Captain Nevin. The fourth was used as a surgery. Bachelors' Hall was the scene of most of the revelries at Fort Victoria and much of Victoria's early social life.

Above Bachelors' Hall, a small school was run by the Reverend R.J. Staines and his wife, alongside their own quarters. On occasion the children up above would pour water down through the cracks and holes in the floor and onto the men below, no doubt in an effort to quiet them when things became a little rowdy.

By the summer of 1851, a private residence had been built for the Douglas family. It was away from the fort on the shores of James Bay, on the site now occupied by the Royal British Columbia Museum and Archives complex. Amelia Douglas was delighted to finally have her own home in which to raise her family. Her thirteenth child was born in 1854; only six of the Douglas children survived to adulthood.

Dr. Helmcken had by that time fallen in love with the oldest Douglas daughter, Cecilia. This happened soon after his arrival at Fort Victoria when he spotted her through an open door leading to James Douglas's office. Later, he described the moment he first saw her. She was, he wrote, as active as a little squirrel, and one of the prettiest objects he had ever seen. She was short, graceful, and, in his eyes, very pretty, with a dark complexion and lovely black eyes. The doctor wrote in his *Reminiscences* that he was more or less captivated by her.

Their courtship was typically Victorian—very proper and circumspect and always chaperoned, consisting of evenings spent "drinking hot chocolate and singing," with appropriately early hours being kept.[7] The doctor pointed out that Cecilia's mother, Amelia, was "awfully jealous" and liked to keep her children close to her. To begin with, therefore, his courtship was not welcomed. All five Douglas girls, Cecilia, Jane, Agnes, Alice, and Martha, were shy, and dominated by their loving but over-protective mother.

When it was finally agreed that Helmcken could marry Cecilia, James Douglas gave them land next door to where his own house stood. A crofter, mechanic, and odd-job builder, Gideon Halcrow, was assigned the task of building the house, which still stands today in its original location.

The wedding date was brought forward at the request of the bride's father, who was planning to leave on a dangerous mission in January 1853. He was pursuing a Cowichan Indian and the son of a Nanaimo chief accused of murdering a company shepherd in the Lake Hill area. James Douglas wanted to be sure his daughter was happily married before he left, in the event that he did not return. Helmcken was only too happy to oblige, and the wedding date was fixed for December 27, 1852. It took place inside the fort, and the ceremony was performed by the Reverend Staines.

As the house being built for the newly married couple was not finished, they temporarily moved into Governor Blanshard's house on the corner of Government and Yates streets. There they were given two rooms and a kitchen, and an Indian named Dick acted as their servant. Dick was paid "two blankets and a shirt per month and Indian provisions occasionally" for his trouble.[8]

The tradition of family life was very important to James and Amelia Douglas, and this tradition was continued through the lives of all of their children within their own marriages.

Martha was the youngest and perhaps most attractive of the Douglas girls; she later became the wife of Dennis Harris. Extraordinarily revealing letters were written by James Douglas to Martha between 1872 and 1874, while she was in England, having been sent there by her father to "get rid of the cobwebs of colonial training and give [her] a proper finish."[9] With typical Victorian patriarchal guidance, Douglas instructed his daughter from afar, telling her frequently how much she was missed at home, though at the same time insisting upon a high standard of conduct.

Frequently, the blatant hypocrisy of Victorian life also crept between the lines of those letters. For instance, Douglas reprimanded his daughter for referring to resting her "weary legs" when it would have been "nicer and more appropriate" to say "weary limbs." He continued: "I wish you to be in all respects ladylike, both in speech and manner. A lady never uses slang phrases, which are essentially vulgar, and to me unbearable." Douglas also reminded her to keep up with her studies even though he wanted her to enjoy her trip. "Arithmetic must not be neglected; no art is more necessary or useful in the daily affairs of life."

When Martha requested a side trip to Paris, her father was adamant: "It might improve your manners by associating with kind, easy, engaging French girls. But there is one strong objection, which I cannot overcome: that is the dread of French morals and sentiment which I believe to be so different from our own. It may be bigotry on my part, their moral sentiments may be as pure as our own, but still the impression remains unchanged in my mind." These comments clearly reveal a standard of morals set by Victorian patriarchs that was, in turn, agreed upon and almost always upheld by their children.

In the summer of 1874, James Douglas decided to visit Martha in England, perhaps to reassure himself that all was well. They later returned home together, after prolonged visiting in both England and Scotland.

By far the most interesting and scandalous story concerning the five Douglas girls was the elopement of Alice Douglas in August 1861. This episode in Douglas family life was a definite departure from the norm.

When she was only seventeen, Alice impulsively ran off with Charles Good, son of the Reverend Henry Good. They were married by an American justice of the peace aboard the British schooner *Explorer* at Port Townsend, but upon their return to Victoria, Douglas insisted on their undergoing a second marriage ceremony, to make sure the union was legal. He was far from happy about his daughter's marriage and would have preferred to have it annulled. Realizing that the union had already been consummated, he decided to make the best of it.

His predictions that the relationship would turn out badly were proved correct. A few years later, after having had three children together, the couple decided to part, he to England and Alice to San Francisco, where she obtained an American divorce and then remarried. The English courts did not recognize the divorce, so Good agreed to apply for a divorce himself. James Douglas later commented that "had she trusted her father more, and put less faith in Good, how different, and how much more happy, would her lot in life have been."[10]

James and Amelia's only son, James, also caused his father much grief. He was sent to England at an early age for an education, which his father thought essential if his son were to succeed in life. Douglas once commented that James was "a child of many cares, the only one out of a family of 13 who is not in the enjoyment of robust health." This was a surprising remark considering that seven of his children died in infancy and two of the six who did survive lived only into their thirties.

Douglas had high hopes for his son and once remarked in a letter to one of his sons-in-law, A.G. Dallas, "I have reproved him for his many boyish projects of going to sea in a merchant marine, becoming a farmer etc., which would be altogether inconsistent with my plans."[11]

As a typical Victorian father, James Douglas frequently reproached his son in correspondence, and, because so many of the Douglas letters survived, there remains today a revealing chronology of the conflicts that existed between father and son while young James was in England. On one occasion, for instance, he cautioned his son about an unwise "emotional entanglement" with a certain young lady. On another, he informed him,

> there is no royal road to learning: It is impossible for anyone to get on, and make his mark in the world, without plenty of hard work. You have a great deal yet to learn. I wish you to write a better hand and a less slovenly letter; you must study composition to express your ideas neatly and clearly.[12]

James junior was obviously a disappointment to his father, who frequently pointed out moral lessons as examples for his son to live by. Victorian fathers took it upon themselves to control and dictate their sons' paths in life and, despite the occasional rebellion, sons usually obeyed.

In the Douglas family, however, father and son never seemed to reconcile their differences. James returned to Victoria in 1870, went into public life, and was eventually elected to the legislature. He later married the daughter of the Honourable A.C. Elliott, the fourth premier of BC, and had two sons, John and James. He died at the age of thirty-two in 1883.

In 1869, news arrived to brighten the Douglas household. The Supreme Court of Canada ruled that Amelia Douglas's father's first marriage to the Cree woman, Miyo Nipiy, had in fact been valid, so his second marriage to Julia Woolrich was null and void. This news finally freed Amelia of her illegitimate status and seemed to bring her out of her shell, enabling her to take a more active role in her husband's affairs.

In the past she had seldom been seen in public. She had been reclusive while the law courts in eastern Canada were considering the appeal made by her brother to contest their father's will and claim his share of William Connolly's estate. Once Miyo Nipiy's legitimacy was proven and the news reached Victoria, Amelia was a changed person. She began to entertain in her home and was even seen out in public.

Possibly the most rewarding aspect of the court's decision was that it enabled Amelia to take pride in her heritage. In later life, she enjoyed relating Indian legends to her grandchildren and once invited a Songhee chief to visit her home.

By that time, Douglas had retired. He had enjoyed his travels through Europe and had returned to Victoria looking forward to a few more years of contentment. He always took a daily walk and frequently drove around Victoria and surrounding areas. He enjoyed reading, smoking his pipe, and, especially, he loved to be with his family. At Amelia's request, he smoked only outside on the front veranda.

Douglas liked to be thought of as the patriarchal figurehead of his family and, despite a stern, dignified, and somewhat cold outward appearance, he was also a man of compassion. He had risen from company employee to chief factor, from governor of Vancouver Island (succeeding Richard Blanshard) to governor of the Crown Colony of BC. He had been knighted by Queen Victoria and had received accolades and praise from around the empire.

His death in 1877 came swiftly and without pain as he sat talking with his son-in-law, having earlier complained of mild chest pains. Victoria mourned his passing, and the funeral given to the grand old man far surpassed any seen before in the city.

Lady Amelia Douglas outlived her husband by thirteen years. She continued to enjoy the simple pleasures of life, surrounded by her children and grandchildren. Members of the Douglas family lived in the family residence for another ten years. In 1902 an auction of family furniture was held, and a few years later the old house was torn down.

The Douglas family can be considered the founders of early social life in Victoria. In particular, James Douglas's personal character traits became firmly imprinted in the lives of those who lived at the fort. His standards of behaviour became the law, and he was responsible for the way Victoria's social life and behaviour began and evolved as the city grew. It is relatively easy to understand how, despite his own somewhat questionable start in life, Douglas took it upon himself to head up that so-called aristocracy in early Victoria, and how his attitudes and principles came to form the basis of future class distinctions.

With a population in the beginning of little more than two hundred, and no other guidelines to show them the way, the first colonists gladly embraced a set of social standards by which to live. Thrown together in unusual circumstances, and relatively isolated from the rest of the world, men and women who perhaps would not otherwise have considered spending time together were suddenly obliged to live side by side. The Douglas law, tied irrevocably to company principles, appeared to them to be a sound and effective way of life.

But nothing lasts forever. In his *Reminiscences*, Dr. Helmcken remarked on the changing social scene that was already happening in the 1850s following the arrival of the farming families sent out by the PSAC:

> The arrival of such nice people altered matters amazingly. There were English ladies . . . rara avis . . . very pleasing and nice. No longer had the officers to look to themselves for amusements. Visits—little teas—occasional parties, or amateur theatricals, or a ball in the messroom took place : . . so life became extended, more artificial and more expensive.[13]

That "extended, more artificial and more expensive" life can be seen through one of those PSAC families—the Skinners.

# The Skinner Family

Left to right: Mary, Thomas with Ada, Annie, Mrs. Skinner with Emily, and Constance.
IMAGE B-00182 COURTESY OF ROYAL BC MUSEUM, BC ARCHIVES

Thomas Skinner [was] . . . a genial gentleman, a sort of liberal conservative, Bailiff of the Puget Sound Company's farm at Esquimalt. He liked the smell of fox and to follow the hounds; but preferred this to being the fox.
—*The Reminiscences of Dr. John Sebastian Helmcken*, ed. Blakey Smith

One evening toward the end of May in 1864, Thomas Skinner sat at his oak desk in the library at Oaklands, his home for the past eleven years.

He gazed out of the window at the sloping land leading down to the cove and the waters of Esquimalt, and thought again about the momentous decision he had recently made. Tomorrow he would be leaving this all behind: the house, his wife's beloved garden, the giant oaks under which his children had played, and all six hundred acres of rich, fertile farmland he had grown to love with a passion.

When he had uprooted his family from England back in 1852, he had thought that once settled in the new colony, he would never again have to dramatically change the lives of his loved ones. That move had been a good one and he had established an excellent life for them all at Oaklands. But now the time had come for more change. It had proved necessary to move on once again and he wondered, for perhaps the hundredth time, whether he was making the right decision.

He sighed as he picked up his elegant, gold-rimmed spectacles and placed them firmly on the end of his nose, curling the rather fragile wire loops securely behind his ears. The wording on the velvet spectacle case, which read "T. Rubergall, Optician to His Majesty, of Coventry, London," was yet another reminder from his past. Similarly, an old, gold-embossed invitation card propped against his inkwell reminded him of a happy occasion from his more recent past when Admiral Bruce of the Royal Navy had "requested the pleasure of the company of Thomas and Mary Skinner" to dinner aboard the *Monarch*. "A boat will be in waiting at 5:30." Would such occasions still be a part of his family's life once they had removed themselves to the unchallenged wilderness of the Cowichan Valley, he wondered?

Two days later, the gunboat *Grappler* carried the Skinners away to that new life in the remote settlement. Thomas Skinner need not have concerned himself about his decision. It turned out to be a good one, and he soon established a new and prosperous life once again for his family in the Cowichan area. His children would all marry well, especially his daughter Constance, who was destined to become the wife of BC's seventh premier, Alexander Edmond Batson Davie.

# CHAPTER TWO

# *Alas! Poor Bastion*

Thomas Skinner and his family arrived in Victoria aboard the *Norman Morison* in the middle of a vicious snowstorm in January 1853.

The Skinners were one of the families sponsored by the Puget Sound Agricultural Company (a subsidiary of the Hudson's Bay Company) to establish a farming community in the colony. This was the time in Victoria's history when solidarity of family roots was needed if colonization were to succeed; these families would eventually become the rural gentry. Thomas Skinner and Kenneth McKenzie, who arrived at the same time, were appointed bailiffs in charge of two farms in Esquimalt. They both brought their families with them, as well as twenty-five other families of carpenters, blacksmiths, farmers, labourers, and servants, who were all needed to work the land.

People like the Skinners and the McKenzies were specifically chosen to be the colony's new blood because of their satisfactory and stable backgrounds. It was felt that they would easily meet the requirements for a respectable establishment on Vancouver Island.

Thomas Skinner's background was more than adequate. His roots could be traced back to Sir Robert Skinner (or Skenner), a Norman knight who had arrived in England with William the Conqueror. Apparently William highly favoured this Skinner and rewarded him greatly, possibly because of a family connection with William's mother, Charlotte, the only daughter of King Edmund II of England. Sir Robert Skinner further improved his station in life by marrying a wealthy heiress of the Bolingbroke family of Lincolnshire. In the year 1350, a Skinner descendant also known as Robert married another heiress and moved to Essex, thereby starting the line from which Thomas Skinner was descended.

Thomas Skinner himself came from West Thurrock in Essex, and prior to his appointment by the PSAC had been employed by the East India Company. West Thurrock is in marshy country alongside the River Thames and was at one time a most picturesque village. The Skinners lived there in a comfortable home with elegant grounds.

Skinner's position with the successful English branch of the East India Company had given him the prestige necessary to be a prospective Vancouver Island colonist. In 1852 he had been approached by officials of the PSAC in London and offered a position as a farm bailiff in Esquimalt. Passage was arranged aboard the *Norman Morison*, and it was just the kind of adventure Skinner relished. He was assured that comfortable accommodation awaited him and his family in Victoria.

According to the diary of Robert Melrose, a carpenter contracted to work in the colony for five years under Kenneth McKenzie, the voyage of the *Norman Morison* was anything but ordinary. The McKenzies and their entourage had boarded at Granton, a port on the Firth of Forth. The Skinners joined the vessel in August 1852 at the East India Docks in London. Rounding Cape Horn the passengers were subjected to a hurricane lasting four days, and their approach to Vancouver Island was equally devastating. It was no wonder that following each near-disaster at sea, Melrose had noted in his diary, "Grog for all hands." For nearly two weeks, the captain tried in vain to negotiate the *Norman Morison*'s approach to the island. Finally, a change of wind to a light westerly enabled him to sail up the Strait of Juan de Fuca and cast anchor in the shelter of the Royal Roads.

The Skinners and their fellow passengers had suffered greatly through those five, long, gruelling months at sea, and now they all felt a sense of regret at having left their homes behind them. The excited anticipation of a new life had long since disappeared and in its place was numb reality.

In addition, Thomas's wife, Mary, was in the last month of pregnancy with her sixth child and would have dearly loved the comfort of a warm bed that did not constantly roll back and forth. To enable his wife to rest, Thomas decided not to disembark immediately but to remain aboard overnight. Next morning, he and his family set off for the fort and found to their horror that no preparations had been made for their arrival. It seemed to have escaped the HBC's attention that over fifty people would suddenly be added to Victoria's population. The McKenzies, who had left the ship the night before, had been offered overcrowded accommodation with other families in a loft inside the fort, and there was no room for the Skinners the next day.

An empty, one-room shack was found for them on what was then known as Kanaka Row (now Humboldt Street). Some Native people were hurriedly called together to sweep it out using fir boughs for brooms, and Hudson's Bay blankets were strung across the room to separate the Skinners' accommodation from that of their servants. It was a dreadful first impression of life in the young colony.

One of the Skinners' maids had received a marriage proposal aboard the *Norman Morison* that, at the time, she had turned down. After spending one night in the miserable shack, she decided to accept the proposal and return to England. Even the prospect of facing another five months at sea was obviously better than life as a servant in that cold land.

Mary and Thomas Skinner were also disturbed by their new surroundings, but their determination and strength of character showed in the way they decided to make the best of these initial catastrophes. And, one month later, in that shack, Mary Skinner gave birth to her sixth child, a healthy girl they called Constance Langford Skinner.

By then, the company was making an attempt to put things right for the Skinners by beginning the construction of a house for them on land later known as Constance Cove Farm. The farm was situated partially in the area where HMCS Naden stands today. The land was fertile and bordered by the sea, and with the hills and mountains as a backdrop, the Skinners' home slowly took shape. It was built on a rolling slope cleared of many oak trees, which gave it its name, Oaklands. With a southern exposure, it stood overlooking a sheltered bay later known as Skinner's Cove. Today that area houses the Esquimalt Graving Dock.

Oaklands was a one-storey structure, twin-gabled and solidly built. It was large and spacious and easily accommodated the ever-growing Skinner family. Two more children were born there. There were nine Skinner children in all, although one son, Francis, had died two years before they left England. The other sons born in England were Ambrose, Robert, and Ernest. The two eldest Skinner girls, Annie and Mary, were also born in England, and Constance was the third daughter.

Ada and Emily were born later at Oaklands and were both christened on board naval ships: Ada (named Ada Jane Bruce to honour Admiral Bruce) in his flagship, HMS *Monarch*, with Captain and Mrs. Langford as her godparents, and Emily aboard HMS *Satellite*, with Captain Prevost as her godfather.

The Skinners and other Puget Sound farming families, like the McKenzies and the already established Langfords, were all closely associated with the naval base in Esquimalt. Their social activities largely centred on the comings and goings of naval vessels. These connections had evolved from the desire of the colonists to hear all the current news of their homeland. By maintaining a social rapport with visiting naval officers, they could also keep in touch with what was happening in the old world. In addition, and perhaps even more importantly, young naval officers presented a very eligible marriage market for the settlers' daughters.

When the Skinners first moved into Oaklands, they were surrounded by dense forest. Their nearest neighbours, the McKenzies, who were now living at Craigflower Farm, were two miles away along a forest trail. Midway between the two farms lay the ancient Indian village of Chachimutupusas. For the most part the village was deserted in favour of the newer Songhee village in Victoria Harbour, but the occasional Indian still frequented the trail and alarmed the Skinners. Mary Skinner had good reason to be nervous; an earlier experience with some Haidas had remained in her mind.

The Haidas, "possibly because of the greater strength and vigour of the northern Indians," had been employed by the company to clear the Skinner land in the early days.[14] They often came from the Queen Charlotte Islands to trade at Fort Victoria, but as they seemed "fierce and untamed" and not nearly as friendly as the local Songhee people, they were inevitably more feared.[15]

Mary Skinner's unfortunate experience with the Haida had occurred on the day when their pay was due. As was the usual custom, they paddled their canoes to the fort and demanded their pay in blankets, the way the HBC always paid its Indian employees. On that day, there were not enough blankets in the supply room, so they were told to return on another day.

The Haida believed they had been the victims of a trick and would not get the pay they deserved, so they canoed back to Skinner's Cove where they held an angry council-of-war. They considered that Thomas Skinner was responsible for the dilemma, since it was his land that they had cleared, and as revenge, they planned to kidnap his children.

Mary Skinner's Songhee nursemaid overheard their plans and quickly ran back to the house with the children to report to her mistress. Mary immediately began to strip the blankets from their own beds and gather together some trinkets. She then told the children to stay together in the house and not make a sound. They were to bolt all the doors as soon as she and the nursemaid left. The young Indian girl was to act as interpreter in the meeting Mary anticipated with the angry Native employees.

She met the Haida at the shore and told them she had brought presents of her own blankets and later they would be paid in full by the company. The Haida were impressed with Mary's pleasant manner and began to gather around her, telling the nursemaid that Mary Skinner was now "their very good friend." The danger was past.

Over the following months, the entire six-hundred-acre Skinner farm was gradually cleared and the forest replaced by open fields ready for planting. The Skinners shared a boundary with Craigflower Farm, and they became firm friends with the McKenzies. Picnics and occasional visits to the farms by James and Amelia Douglas were highlights, as were boating jaunts up the Gorge waterway.

As the farms continued to prosper, the PSAC decided to build two large warehouses on the north shore of Skinner's Cove, turning the waterfront of Skinner's land into a loading and unloading dock for HBC vessels and Russian ships. Wheat, flour, beef, and other farm produce were profitably traded. The warehouses remained there until 1924 when they were demolished to make room for the Dominion Graving Dock.

By its second year of operation, the Skinner farm was producing good crops of wheat, barley, potatoes, and turnips, and had a large herd of cattle. In 1854 theirs was the only farm selling butter; they had erected nine houses and had a population of thirty-four. In addition, Thomas Skinner obtained a contract at the time of the Crimean War to supply beef from Esquimalt for Her Majesty's Fleet.

The Skinner children grew up in a happy home environment and their unfortunate arrival was soon forgotten. All the children owned their own ponies. They had been taught to ride on a horse that was once apparently owned by the infamous Fraser River outlaw Ned McGowan, and they named their horse in his honour.

Early pioneer life for children was full of simple, unsophisticated pleasures, and the Skinner children's amusements were typical. A trip up the Gorge in canoes under the supervision of the Reverend Staines was a special delight. Another was watching the many ceremonies performed by the Native people, a fascination for the children of the fort and farming families. And when there was nothing else to do, they could always count on the spectacle of a seaman being whipped for some misdemeanour. On the days when naval vessels arrived in the harbour loaded with toys, oranges, and even firecrackers, the children had a great deal to enjoy.

The children at the fort could even earn money trapping the rats that were abundant in the dormitories. Or, as one youngster put it, it was equally pleasurable "just lying at full length thinking of the beautiful country" in which they lived.[16]

Thomas and Mary Skinner were hospitable people and enjoyed entertaining at Oaklands. Most of their dinner guests were visiting naval officers or colonists like themselves who were becoming interested in the politics of the colony. Thomas Skinner was appointed justice of the peace in March 1853. Such appointments were usually made as a result of social standing in the colony. Nevertheless, even though Skinner and his colleagues McKenzie and Langford were all well-educated men, James Douglas apparently considered them "ignorant and unreliable." Thomas Skinner was becoming a man of independent thought, and there was much he disagreed with concerning company policy; this may have been the reason for Douglas's remark.

When elections were held for the first legislative assembly in August 1856, Skinner, along with Dr. John Helmcken, was elected to represent the district of Esquimalt and Metchosin. About this time, Skinner began to openly criticize the company and all those in authority. He was becoming more interested in the affairs of the Esquimalt area and campaigned strongly in August 1860 for "the important necessity for steps being taken to repair the road and bridges leading to Esquimalt, a road which it is well known is more traveled over and of more importance than any other road in the country."[17]

In February 1861, Thomas Skinner became involved in the organization of a Vancouver Island display to be exhibited at an industrial exhibition in London, in company with Governor Douglas, Bishop Hills, Bishop Demers, Judge Begbie, Dr. Helmcken, and others of equal importance in the colony. It is apparent that Skinner was by then moving in high circles. In support of the exhibition, Skinner reported to the assembly that in 1854 he had sent home a sample of wheat and, in reply, had received a letter stating that the specimen of wheat was "the finest ever grown in any country."

In keeping with his independent nature, by August 1861 he was leading what the *Colonist* described as an "indignation meeting" at Williams Saloon in Esquimalt, to "take into consideration the way in which the Government had given out the contract for the new road."[18]

The time, however, was not right for clashing with the governing company. Although things were changing, it was unwise to completely dissociate oneself from the protection of the company umbrella. When the PSAC's assets were taken over by the HBC, Skinner finally decided he should move on. He had earlier purchased land in the Cowichan district, and in 1864 he uprooted his family from Esquimalt and moved to Cowichan to begin life again as an independent farmer in the valley.

It was a bold move, for the Skinner family had grown accustomed to their comfortable life at Oaklands. Their social status was established. Their numerous gatherings included balls, riding parties, concerts, and shipboard dances, and a constant stream of social activity took place in their home.

However, in May 1864, the *Colonist* reported:

The gunboat *Grappler* carried to Cowichan yesterday, Thomas J. Skinner and family who, after a residence of many years in the vicinity of Esquimalt, have been obliged to give up their old home and begin life anew in a remote settlement.[19]

"Remote" was an adequate description of Cowichan in those days. There was little to recommend it as a settlement. According to the Skinner children, it was a hard pioneering existence. Their new life in the valley began in tents while they waited for their log cabin to be built. A shortage of sawmills nearby meant long delays in the supply of lumber but, with the determined spirit of Thomas and Mary Skinner, it was not long before the family was once again established as an important part of a community.

Later, they managed to build a finer, more comfortable home, which they called Farleigh. The Skinner children helped with the farming chores of milking the cows and churning the butter. The following September, the first of the Skinner daughters was married. At seventeen, Annie became the bride of a young naval officer, John Bremner, whom she had first met as a child in Esquimalt. The young couple left the valley soon after their marriage and returned to England.

Constance, the daughter born in the shack on the outskirts of Fort Victoria, envied her older sister. She would also have dearly loved to leave the Cowichan Valley. Her heart still held happy memories of life at Oaklands, full of interesting visitors. She had revelled in the lively discussions between her father and visiting politicians and naval officers, and she greatly missed the times when important decisions were made during dinner or in the library over port and cigars. Although she had then been a child, she never forgot the thrill and excitement of those evenings.

Eventually, Constance did leave the valley and for her it was to return to an even more prestigious social life in Victoria. Early in the 1870s, she met and fell in love with a handsome young Victoria lawyer, Alexander Edmond Batson Davie, a man destined for an important place in British

Columbia politics. Their marriage in December 1874 united two very important families in the colony's early establishment.

The Davie family had arrived on Vancouver Island in 1862 when Alexander was a boy of sixteen. His father, John Chapman Davie, was one of Victoria's first physicians and a member of the early legislature. He later practised medicine in the Cowichan Valley and there he became a well-loved and respected member of the community.

There were four Davie sons, two of whom, Alexander and Theodore, became premiers of the province. Another, named after their father, went into medicine. This son took over his father's practice in Cowichan, was later appointed provincial public health officer, and became most famous as an early promoter of Lord Lister's antiseptic surgical methods at both the Royal Jubilee and St. Joseph's hospitals in Victoria. He also created something of a sensation when he eloped in July 1884 with Sarah Todd, the daughter of Victoria salmon-canning magnate Jacob Hunter Todd. In May 1874, Theodore was at the centre of equally startling news when he married a fourteen-year-old girl named Blanche Eliza Baker.

The marriage between Constance Skinner and Alexander Davie was performed by the Reverend David Holmes at the bride's home, Farleigh. By the time Alexander was thirty, he had been elected a member of the legislature for the Cariboo and in 1877 he became a cabinet minister.

Constance loved her new life, married to an up-and-coming politician and lawyer in Victoria. The young couple built an elegant home on Michigan Street, and it became the meeting place for all the politicians of the day.

From the many hours Constance had spent as a child listening to political discussions, she had learned a great deal. Now, as the wife of Alexander Davie, she was able to join knowledgeably in the political soirées on Michigan Street. Unlike some women, she refused to stay in the background. Instead, she spoke her mind in a forthright and intelligent manner, supporting her husband's often controversial views. Possibly she was the driving force behind his success as he climbed the political ladder to become premier of the province on the death of Premier Smithe in 1887. Constance Davie's role was an unusual one. It was not common for women to be involved in matters of a political nature—women were thought of as mere appendages to their husband's careers.

Alexander Davie also held the position of Attorney General, but two years later, at the young age of forty-three, he suddenly died. It was a tragic end to a brief but brilliant career. Constance was comforted in her loss by her strong religious beliefs. She and her husband had converted to the Roman Catholic faith seven years earlier, and Constance remained a devout member of that church for the rest of her life.

The Davies had three sons and four daughters, but only one of their sons survived infancy. Following Alexander's death, Constance continued to live on Michigan Street with her son, Frank, and daughters Emily, Winnifred, Ethel, and Clare. In 1896, Emily married the senior member of the legal firm of McPhillips, Wooton and Barnard.

By involving herself in her children's lives and furthering her own already established position as a hostess of note, Constance easily retained her reputation as political chatelaine. Her parents always enjoyed their visits to the Michigan house and were proud of their daughter's success.

The same year that Alexander died, Constance's father, Thomas, also died, at sixty-seven. Mary Skinner lived on at Farleigh until her own death in 1896. Both Thomas and Mary Skinner are buried in St. Peter's Church at Quamichan.

Constance and Alexander Davie's only son, C.F. Davie, became speaker of the house when Tolmie was premier and, like his father, was a member of the legal profession. The Davie daughters all married well into the legal or political scene, thereby retaining a strong family tradition of law and politics down through the generations in BC. Of the other children of Thomas and Mary Skinner, Robert also became successful as a provincial inspector of timber. Descendants of Ada Jane Bruce Skinner still live in Victoria.

The Skinners, however, were the last of that old school. By the beginning of the 1860s, a change was already taking place in Victoria, marking the end of the old lifestyle established under company rule. And, almost as a symbol of that change, the *Colonist* of December 15, 1860, noted, with a touch of nostalgia, that

> The old picket fence that has so long surrounded the fort yard is fast disappearing. Piece after piece it is taken down, sawed up, and piled away for firewood. Yesterday afternoon workmen commenced removing the old bastion at the corner of View and Government streets, and before today's sun gilds the western horizon, the wood comprising it will no doubt have shared the ignoble fate of the unfortunate pickets. Alas! poor bastion. Thy removal should be enough to break the heart of every Hudson Bay man in the country.[20]

Just as those old pickets went down to their "ignoble fate," so too did the early social life of Victoria. Once successfully implemented, surveyor Pemberton's town plan began to invite settlers, radically changing Victoria's social scene. The simple life of Fort Victoria, as well as of the surrounding rural communities, was slowly disappearing. Even Douglas's social values were being challenged, but the establishment of the first farming families, successfully creating a definitely English country atmosphere in the colony, had managed to extend the foundation of colonial life.

Now, something new was in the wind.

# The Pemberton Family

Children of Frederick Bernard Pemberton and Mary Ann Dupont Bell. Left to right:
Philippa Despard, Frederick Despard (d. 1917), Warren Colclough (d. 1916),
Armine Morris (d. 1960). In the garden of Gonzales on the occasion of the
wedding of Hugo Robert Walter Beaven to Ada Pemberton, September 1902.

Joseph Pemberton, Surveyor General, who always endeavoured to induce
both sides to agree! *In medio tutissima*, his motto.

> —*The Reminiscences of Dr. John Sebastian
> Helmcken*, ed. Blakey Smith

The booming of cannon announced their arrival in March 1864.

Joseph and Teresa Pemberton, newly wed, were well aware that the pomp and ceremony surrounding the approach of the *Brother Jonathan* was not for them. Among their fellow passengers from England was the new governor of Vancouver Island, Arthur Edward Kennedy, his wife, and two pretty daughters, and they were the centre of all the attention.

Kennedy, a retired British army officer, had an Irish background that initially had endeared him to Pemberton, who had similar roots. Most people were now wondering how the new governor would adapt to the social structure of the raw, young colony he was about to lead.

When the *Brother Jonathan* arrived in Esquimalt Harbour, the party was transferred to the gunboat *Grappler* for the final leg of the long journey to Victoria, and Teresa Pemberton realized that she was more concerned with how *she* would adapt. She was, after all, of very distinguished birth, being one of the German Grautoffs and the granddaughter of Justinius Ritze of Baireuth, who had served under no less than Princess Wilhelmina herself. Teresa carried her heritage well with an inborn aristocratic, elegant bearing. German society, of which her parents had been a part, was often austere and solemn, but at the same time had a certain magnificence. Would the colony of Vancouver Island, about which her new husband had written such glowing reports, hold charms for her?

She recalled her first meeting with Joe Pemberton in London and their mutual attraction. She had avidly read his *Facts and Figures Relating to Vancouver Island*. His writings were considered to be exceptional, and many said that his descriptive words equalled his talents and skills as a surveyor. He had a remarkable grasp of the location and the times; much later his book would be described as a "literary gem."

But, at that time, Teresa Jane Pemberton was so in love with Joe that she did not need any convincing as to his abilities. She already knew he was destined for great things. Together they would, she felt sure, carve a place for themselves in the history of the province.

And she was, of course, quite right.

# CHAPTER THREE

## In a Tin Canister

Joseph Despard Pemberton, Vancouver Island's first surveyor general, wrote in 1860 in his *Facts and Figures Relating to Vancouver Island* that "persons emigrating frequently form too high anticipations of becoming suddenly wealthy; . . . and become too soon disappointed." His book was Vancouver Island's first real promotional work and was intended to attract more people from the British Isles.

Pemberton was a wise man. He knew the pitfalls of emigration and he understood, perhaps better than most, the dreams and aspirations held by those who ventured into the unknown. His excellent survey work, followed by his new town plan for Victoria, would undoubtedly attract a new breed of colonist. He believed that many of this new breed would reason that "because they [had] failed in everything they undertook at home, the time had come to repair their fortunes abroad. Never was there a greater fallacy." Instead, he wanted every colonist to face reality, for he knew they would find strong competition and it would be necessary to work even harder to succeed in the new world.

Harriet Sampson, one of Pemberton's daughters, later wrote an article about her famous father, "My Father, Joseph Despard Pemberton: 1821–93." In it, she tells a little of his background and her words paint a clear picture not only of the man himself but also of his Irish roots. They enable the reader to understand how important Pemberton's contribution actually was to colonization.

The name Joseph was a favourite in the Pemberton family. It had been passed down through many generations, beginning with the Right Honourable Joseph Pemberton, Dublin's lord mayor in 1806. That Pemberton produced eighteen sons and three daughters, and one of those sons, also named Joseph, was the father of Vancouver Island's first surveyor. Another of the lord mayor's sons, Augustus Frederick, also achieved a notable career in British Columbia as a Victoria magistrate and county court judge.

Joseph Despard Pemberton was born in Dublin on July 23, 1821, educated at Trinity College, Dublin, and then studied engineering under Sir John McNeill. He was also a student of Sir George Hemans, the principal engineer of the Midland Railway of Ireland. Pemberton progressed steadily, and his talents were soon widely recognized. In subsequent years, he became assistant engineer of the Great Southern and Western Railway and later was chief engineer of the Dublin & Drogheda Railway, as well as the Exeter & Crediton and the East Lancashire railways in England.

In 1850, he entered a prestigious competition to design the building that was to house the International Exhibition of 1851 in London. Although he did not win—the prize went to architect Joseph Paxton for his design, known later as the Crystal Palace—Pemberton was awarded the Prince Albert Bronze Medal for his submission.

Earlier he had accepted a post as professor of surveying, civil engineering, and mathematics at the Royal Agricultural College in Cirencester, Gloucestershire. It would seem, however, that instructing others did not appeal to Pemberton for very long, and he longed to return to more practical work in the field. He therefore began planning the construction of a railway to cross the Isthmus of Suez, and in November 1850 he sent his proposal to the drector general of the Egyptian transit. Although it was not accepted, eight years later an identical plan was adopted.

Instead of pursuing his idea for fieldwork in Egypt, Pemberton decided to leave England and head for undeveloped land on the Pacific. Hearing of the HBC's plans to colonize Vancouver Island and the company's need for a qualified surveyor, one who would be able to prepare maps, make surveys, and supervise the general construction of public works, Pemberton applied for the position and was immediately accepted.

In February 1851, he signed a contract with the HBC, undertaking to serve as colonial surveyor and engineer for three years. As an added incentive, he was given money for his passage out and back, plus a promised bonus of five hundred pounds if his work proved to be satisfactory by the time the agreement expired.

He sailed from Southampton in a regular ship of the Royal Mail Steam Packet Company. His ocean journey was uneventful, but crossing the Isthmus of Panama in the days before the railway was a perilous ordeal and one he did not soon forget. He later wrote of the experience: "Who that crossed it then can forget the heat and filth of Chagres, the packs of curs and flocks of buzzards, the struggle in bungos and with boatmen up the river, the scenes of riot and debauchery at the villages, jungle fever, and the bones that marked the mule tracks through the plains of Panama, and stamped the short but fatal route of fifty miles, as the Golgotha of the West?"[21]

He contracted malaria and was forced to interrupt his journey until he recovered. He reached San Francisco in April 1851 and Fort Vancouver, on the Columbia River, one month later. By the end of June, he was installed at Fort Victoria. Joseph Pemberton's early surveying of Vancouver Island is clearly documented in correspondence between James Douglas and the Colonial Office in London. His first assignment was a preliminary survey of the island's coastline. Next, he surveyed and mapped the fur trade reserve, the land around the fort retained by the HBC for its own purposes. All this work was completed by November of Pemberton's first year in the colony.

Soon afterward, the HBC decided that to further the cause of colonization, a suitable townsite should be laid out.

Before year's end, Douglas approached his surveyor with a request for plans for townsites beside the fort and also on Esquimalt Harbour. In January 1852, Douglas was able to report that he was forwarding by the *Norman Morison* "a Tin Canister . . . containing a plan of the Town of Victoria."[22]

Pemberton's next two surveys involved trips out to Saanich plus a journey into the wilderness of Cowichan. He was, in fact, the first white man to venture that far at that time. By March, a second tin canister, full of maps showing his discoveries, had been received in London.

Between 1853 and 1855, Pemberton surveyed the island from Sooke to Nanaimo, and his findings and subsequent maps were both accurate and interesting. His contract with the company should have expired in June 1854, but early that year Douglas recommended to London that Pemberton's services be retained. The company agreed and, in July, a letter from company secretary Archibald Barclay was sent to Pemberton:

> I am directed by the Governor and Committee . . . with reference to your engagement with the Company . . . to inform you they are so much satisfied with the zeal and talent which you have shewn during the time you have been connected with the Company, that they will be happy to retain your services.[23]

Before the new contract was drawn up, Pemberton was given his promised bonus plus the offer of a substantial salary increase over the next three years and travelling expenses for a trip back to England. A living allowance was also granted to him, in place of board and lodging at the fort.

In October 1855, Pemberton signed his new agreement, after having made a visit to London for "consultation purposes." While there, he also had his first book, *The South Eastern Districts of Vancouver Island, from a Trigonometrical Survey*, published by John Arrowsmith.

Not only were his talents as a surveyor considerable, he was also a brave and venturesome explorer. In October 1856, he was instructed to explore the land between Qualicum and the Alberni Valley. Crossing the island was a perilous adventure, as was his encounter with the chief of the Nitinat people, who was far from friendly.

Pemberton continued to carry out his duties through wild land and, when he was back in Victoria, he designed and built bridges and a variety of buildings. Douglas also sought his expertise for laying out mainland towns such as Derby, on the site of Fort Langley.

In December 1858, Pemberton's contract expired and he decided to sever his connection with the HBC. The company was handing over the colony of Vancouver Island to the British government, so it would have had no further need of his services. Douglas, however, wanted to retain Pemberton as colonial surveyor and surveyor general, a position he held until 1864.

Thereafter, Pemberton was involved in many projects, from the laying out of roads in Sooke and Saanich to the design and erection of the Race Rocks and Fisgard lighthouses.

His interests in the colony extended to things political. From 1856 to 1859, he was a member of the first legislative assembly of Vancouver Island. In September 1863, he became a member of the executive council of Vancouver Island and the following year of the legislative council. In October that year, he resigned all his appointments, save for that of surveyor general. He returned to the political arena briefly in 1867 to represent the Victoria District on the legislative council and served in that capacity for two years.

Somewhere along the way, Pemberton decided to remain permanently on Vancouver Island. His time here had become more than merely a career experience, and he had gradually grown to love the island and adopt it as his own.

He had first seen the Gonzales area of Victoria in 1855 and had immediately decided to purchase land there. He was enamoured of the gentle slopes, the glorious view of the Olympic Mountains, and the plentiful deer and other wildlife. He obviously felt it was an area where a man could easily settle, but in the beginning, there was only "a log dwelling house 30 x 20 feet, a barn and some small outhouses" on the acreage he purchased.[24]

On the strength of his own feelings about Gonzales, he sent for his sister, Susan, to join him the following year. Susan Pemberton was at first provided with accommodation at the fort, and then she moved with her brother out to his Gonzales property. Soon they began to entertain on a large scale at the small "log house," and their social activities became another central point for their elite group of friends, thus extending once again the boundaries of social life in early Victoria.

The Pembertons' Irish hospitality welcomed friends and acquaintances at numerous dances. The rooms were always ablaze with candles. These candles were placed in potato jackets that served as holders in lieu of wall sconces. When picnics were arranged, old farm horses were commandeered to pull cartloads of guests and baskets full of food. Most picnics took place in the surrounding glades or coastal spots, while the sport of archery was indulged in by ladies and gentlemen alike.

Other activities enjoyed by the Pembertons and their friends were theatricals, concerts, and musical evenings. Well-produced plays, including *The Rivals*, performed at the fort and starring Joseph Pemberton as Sir Lucius O'Trigger, helped to pass the time on long winter evenings.

Susan Pemberton was the principal of Angela College for twelve years. In 1868, she was forced to resign her position and return to England due to ill health. At that time, a letter was written to her by the Standing Committee of the Diocese of British Columbia and the board of management of the college, in which they wished her a speedy recovery. The letter was a staunch testimonial to her contribution to college life, and shows the high esteem in which she was held. It states:

> Accept our grateful thanks for the able and conscientious manner in which you have fulfilled your many and serious responsibilities, our repeated expressions of sincere regret for the cause which has led to your resignation, and our earnest prayer that Almighty God who has hitherto strengthened you in the past may still have you in His holy keeping.[25]

Good wishes were, unfortunately, not enough. Susan Pemberton died at St. Germain in France on April 13, 1870.

Through the years, her brother had made frequent trips to England. In 1860 he had gone to London to complete arrangements for the publishing of his second book, *Facts and Figures Relating to Vancouver Island and British Columbia*, in August of that year.

In 1864 he was again in London, to recuperate following a riding accident he had sustained on the Esquimalt Road. While there, he met and married Teresa Jane Despard Grautoff. Although the name Despard was common to both families, Joseph Pemberton and his bride were not related. Soon after their marriage, the couple left for Vancouver Island, sailing there with Arthur Kennedy, the man who was to become the new governor of BC. The party arrived in Victoria in March 1864, and their arrival was reported in the newspapers of the day:

> Yesterday, at precisely 3 o'clock, the booming of a cannon shot, immediately followed by a second, conveyed to the inhabitants of Victoria the news of the arrival of our new Governor. Every vehicle in the city that could be run, or any kind of locomotive was put into operation and

hurried down to Esquimalt with all haste. There was a naval salute of thirteen guns from the vessels anchored in Esquimalt Harbour.[26]

Although the welcoming committee was not specifically for her, it was an auspicious beginning for Teresa Pemberton as a young bride in the new colony. Joseph, now a happily married man, decided to devote more time to developing his estate at Gonzales while Teresa continued the social traditions her husband and his sister had begun there. With his strong interest in horses, Joseph began importing a well-known Clydesdale breed, the Glengarry, to Vancouver Island, in addition to Percherons and Shorthorn cattle.

His love of horses was later inherited by his son, Joseph, who trained and rode his own horses at the spring and fall meets in Colwood. Much later, these meets would be another excuse for large social gatherings. Anyone interested in such sports would drive out to Colwood carrying the "colours of their favourite riders floating in the breeze."[27] Often, the lieutenant-governor and his party would join the group of socialites and military and naval officers. Following the meet, there would inevitably be a prize-giving ceremony and a large picnic tea.

In 1885, Joseph and Teresa Pemberton built a much larger and more elaborate home on their property. The new Gonzales, which cost ten thousand dollars to complete and stood on the southeast corner of St. Charles and Rockland streets, had twenty elegant rooms, five bathrooms, a billiard room, a conservatory, and a library. It too became a centre where the socially elite gathered for elegant balls, and garden or dinner parties.

Teresa Pemberton, the young bride of 1864, who had experienced the quaint, old-fashioned gatherings of early colonial life when young naval officers had organized riding parties or picnics in Pemberton Woods and Langford, and the ladies had dressed in crinolines and bonnets, had now become the social chatelaine at the new Gonzales. The big house was occupied by members of the Pemberton family until her death in 1916.

Joseph Pemberton himself died suddenly in November 1893, following a heart attack when riding home with his wife from a Hunt Club paper chase. It was a fitting end for a man who had always loved being in the saddle.

During his lifetime, Pemberton achieved a great deal for the colony. As well as his important early survey work, he had founded, in company with his son, Frederick Bernard Pemberton, the firm of Pemberton & Son in 1887. This firm of surveyors, civil engineers, and real estate and financial agents was first located on the site of the Yarrow Building, at the corner of Fort and Broad streets. In 1948 the offices moved to the Holmes block at the corner of Government and Broughton. It was an appropriate move, for it was on that precise spot that Joseph Pemberton had first had an office as colonial surveyor in 1851. Today, the prestigious real estate firm of Pemberton Holmes Ltd. continues to operate from many locations in Victoria.

Joseph and Teresa Pemberton had six children: three sons, Frederick, William, and Joseph, and three daughters, Sophia, Harriet, and Ada.

Frederick Bernard Pemberton, born in 1865, was educated in England and graduated from University College, London, in 1885. He was the son who became co-founder of the real estate firm with his father. He was also a well-known horticulturalist in Victoria and is credited with introducing the first holly to Vancouver Island. Frederick married Mary Ann Dupont Bell in 1893 and the couple had six children. Two of their sons were killed in the First World War, and one of their daughters, by her marriage into the Holmes family, linked those two families in the business enterprise of Pemberton Holmes Ltd. Frederick Pemberton later named his house on Foul Bay Road Mountjoy, in memory of where his great-grandfather, the lord mayor of Dublin, had once lived—Mountjoy Square in that Irish city.

William Parnell Despard Pemberton was born in 1877, also educated in England and graduated in 1899 from Cambridge University. Upon his return to Canada, he earned a Bachelor of Science degree in 1903 from McGill University and was later involved in mining engineering in BC. Joseph's namesake son, Joe, trained and raced his own hunters in steeplechases at Colwood for many years.

Sophia studied art in Paris and London, and her work was exhibited at the Royal Academy. She later became the wife of Canon Beanlands of Christ Church Cathedral. Following the canon's death, Sophia married Horace Deane-Drummond. She died in 1959 at the age of ninety. Harriet, who wrote the article about her famous father, was one of the founders of the Alexandra Club for Women and was also one of The Group of Seven women who helped design and carve the oak reredos behind the altar of St. Mary's Church in Oak Bay. Her earlier travels through Europe had taught her much about wood carvings in European churches. Her husband was W. Curtis Sampson. Ada married Hugo Robert Beavan, a realtor and insurance agent, who was the son of Robert Beavan, an early mayor of Victoria and later premier of BC.

When Joseph Despard Pemberton returned to England in 1855 to bring back his sister Susan to the colony, he also brought with him his favourite uncle, Augustus Frederick Pemberton, and this eventually created a second family of Pembertons. Augustus, also born in Dublin, was only a few years older than his nephew and the two men became close friends. Augustus had agreed to manage a farm in the new colony to be financed by his nephew. Thanks to James Douglas's decision to open up much of the fur trade reserve land previously held by the HBC, many pioneering families, including the Pembertons, were able to buy up enormous acreages at reasonable prices. With land values soaring in later years, most of these people became very wealthy landowners.

For his first two years on Vancouver Island, Augustus Pemberton worked at his nephew's Gonzales estate, clearing land and adding on to the existing buildings. Then, in 1858, he accepted an appointment from James

Douglas as commissioner of police and served as magistrate of the police court, which was then held in the barracks courtroom. In 1861, he married Jane Brew of Galway, Ireland, who had come out to Vancouver Island to act as housekeeper for her brother, Chartres. He had been an officer in the Irish constabulary and had been hired to organize a similar police force in BC.

The marriage of Jane Brew and Augustus Pemberton, performed by Bishop Cridge at Christ Church Cathedral, was a grand affair with a large wedding party that included Martha Douglas, daughter of James and Amelia, as one of the flower girls. This was a sign of the closeness between the Pemberton and Douglas families.

Jane and Augustus had three children: a son, Chartres Cecil (known as C.C.), and two daughters, Augusta and Evaline. Evaline became the first registered nurse in Canada and died in 1965.

Augustus Pemberton died in 1881 at the age of seventy-three, by which time his importance in the colony meant that such people as Judge Matthew Begbie and Roderick Finlayson were pallbearers at his funeral.

The name Pemberton was highly thought of in the colony for many years. At the time of the Confederation dispute, Joseph Pemberton's opinion was listened to and respected. Despite his Irish background, he was a strong supporter and loyal subject of the queen. He was initially horrified to think of Vancouver Island joining the United States and considered such thoughts almost "treasonable." On the other hand, he did not want it to become part of Canada either. Canada was far away in the east, and it was just as foreign, to his way of thinking, as the United States. He would have preferred the colony to remain a British outpost on the Pacific. If, however, BC had to join hands with a greater power, he decided to come down in favour of annexation with the United States. In 1871, when the province's fate was sealed with Canada, Pemberton's views were overruled.

He was, however, first and foremost a gentleman farmer whose life largely revolved not around politics, but around his Gonzales acreage.

There, his charming wife with her regal German background played the graceful hostess and set the scene for future chatelaines such as Caroline O'Reilly and Julia Trutch. The ladies of that early period led leisurely lives, enjoying "... their splendid furniture, rugs, pictures, and bijoux," which arrived from England to give their homes comfort and beauty.[28] Their "gowns and shawls, exquisite laces and other finery, finely tailored riding clothes, all very chic and complete from the hat to the varnished boots," merely added to their somewhat charmed lives.[29]

The name of Pemberton is today perpetuated in many ways throughout the province. In Victoria, Pemberton Road and Mountjoy and Despard avenues run through property that was once part of the Gonzales estate. In addition, Oak Bay Avenue owes its existence to Joseph Pemberton, for he came out of semi-retirement from Gonzales to design it, having earlier surveyed the land where it was eventually built. The placement of the road, the entire length of which passed through his own property, was a clever move, as eventually it opened up and developed an entirely new and very profitable area of Victoria, all to his benefit.

In 1864, the names Pemberton Point and Despard Cove on Broughton Island were bestowed by Captain Pender of the Royal Navy in honour of Joseph Pemberton, and the towns of Pemberton, Pemberton Meadows, and Pemberton Portage in the interior of BC commemorate his early surveys throughout the province.

In addition, as philanthropists, the Pembertons' contributions to Victoria were enormous. Joseph's many generous financial donations through the years included a two thousand dollar bequest in his will for an operating room at the Royal Jubilee Hospital.

It is somewhat ironic that a member of the next subject family in this work once wrote an interesting comment on Joseph Despard Pemberton's book, *Facts and Figures Relating to Vancouver Island and British Columbia*. Lindley Crease referred to the work as "a literary gem," and went on to say:

In this book we find how his mind grasps the vision of the future. He sees the position which this part of the Continent will take in an Empire which was then in course of formation, and for the preservation and building up of which we are in our day like-wise responsible.[30]

Not only was Joseph Pemberton a man of considerable talent and vision, he was a man well loved and respected by his peers. His friend and assistant, Benjamin W. Pearse, described him as "always cheery, bright and sanguine. He was affectionate without ostentation, [and] of a most amiable nature."[31]

He headed up a family lineage whose name, well over a century later, still commands respect. The Pembertons were the beginning of a different kind of gentry, an upper-class group of colonists that extended beyond the confines of fort and company rule, and even beyond the rural aspect of that early privileged life. This new breed of Victoria's aristocracy was destined to continue in the capable hands of families such as the Creases, O'Reillys, and Trutches.

# The Crease Family

Josephine, Lindley, Mary, Arthur, and Susan Crease, 1903.
IMAGE F-06876 COURTESY OF ROYAL BC MUSEUM, BC ARCHIVES

I am deeply impressed with the momentous character of the discussion into which we are about to enter, the grave importance of a decision by which the fate of this our adopted country of British Columbia must be influenced for better, for worse, for all time to come.

—Attorney General H.P. Crease, from "Debate on the Subject of Confederation" of Canada in *Government Gazette Extraordinary*, March/May 1870

When the official letter from Ottawa arrived, it was placed ceremoniously on a silver tray in the grand hall of Pentrelew. There were still signs of Christmas every-where in the house, even though the New Year had been rung in two nights before and it was now early January 1896. Laurel wreaths and greenery adorned the walls and staircase.

A uniformed maid carried the silver tray into the study where she knew she would find Mr. Crease at this time of the day. He was well advanced in years now, well past his three score and ten, but his mind was still alert and he readily gave her a cheerful but formal "Enter" when she knocked. She smiled, placed the letter in front of him, and made a hasty retreat.

Henry Pering Pellew Crease reached for his letter opener. The thick white parchment paper inside the envelope had the royal seal on the top and bore the words "Ottawa, Ontario, January 1st–2nd, 1896."

> It gives me much pleasure to inform you that the Queen approves the bestowal of knighthood upon you on the occasion of your retirement from an honourable judicial career, commencing so many years ago.

Crease's hand shook slightly as he read on. The shaking was partly due to the normal tremors of old age but mostly from excitement and pride he could not hide, despite a rigid upbringing and lifestyle that was not conducive to outbursts of emotion. The letter was signed Aberdeen. He would call Sarah immediately. She would be so proud of him, as would all their children. Three years earlier he had been appointed Deputy Judge in Admiralty of the Exchequer Court of Canada, but his law career in British Columbia had spanned some thirty-eight years. His last day in court would officially be January 17. It had been a long and interesting career; this honour from Ottawa was the icing on the cake.

He clutched the letter to him as he rose slowly. Once the news got out, he knew that many people would be calling at Pentrelew to congratulate him. The house would be full again. He liked it that way. The hustle and bustle of social activities always gave him pleasure.

But first he must go to Sarah and tell her. She would enjoy a quiet moment with him, to contemplate. Sir Henry and Lady Crease—he thought it had a nice ring to it.

# CHAPTER FOUR

# The Prosperous Western Outlet

To this point, the social life of upper-class families in Victoria had been controlled by those in a governing position, those who were farming the land, and those who were surveying it. It was inevitable that sooner or later lawyers would also become involved as part of the social scene.

Henry Pering Pellew Crease, a native of Cornwall, was the lawyer destined to lead the way. Born in August 1823 at Ince Castle, near Plymouth, he was the eldest son of Captain Henry Crease, an officer in the Royal Navy who retired early to manage tin mines for the Duchy of Cornwall. Henry's mother, Mary Smith, was the heiress of Ince Castle and an artist of some note. As a boy, Henry attended Mount Radford School in Exeter and was a contemporary of Joseph Trutch, who would later become British Columbia's first lieutenant-governor.

Henry graduated from Clare College, Cambridge, and was called to the Bar of the Middle Temple in London. After being called to the Upper Bar in 1849, he moved with his family to Toronto hoping to salvage the family fortunes, which had been slowly dwindling. Failing to prosper there, he returned alone to England where Sarah Lindley, his fiancée, was waiting for him.

By 1858, he had decided to try his luck again in Canada, this time in the west. So, at age thirty-five, he came to Victoria, hoping the news he had heard of the Cariboo gold rush was true and that he would soon make his fortune. His wife and three small daughters, Mary, Susan, and Barbara (one son had died in infancy) would come out two years later.

Crease soon made his mark in Victoria, not as a gold seeker but as a lawyer and politician. On December 22, 1859, as his wife and daughters were sailing to join him, an advertisement in the *Colonist* shows that he was already running for election in the House of Assembly:

> I claim your suffrages as a liberal and independent reformer. Every measure that will promote the rapid growth of this promising colony, and foster its real progress, will have my warm support.[32]

In December 1859, he became Victoria's first barrister when he was called to the Bars of British Columbia and Vancouver Island. On October 14, 1861, he also became Attorney General of the Colony of British Columbia, and in 1870 he was made Justice of the Supreme Court.

As a member of the executive council and as Attorney General, Crease was part of the group who drafted the Terms of Union with Canada in 1870, and had opened the notorious debate on the subject of Confederation in March that year. He was well aware of the importance of the occasion, as he felt strongly that Confederation was the only choice for "faithful subjects of the British crown." He emphasized his opinion with these words:

> Our only option is between remaining a petty isolated community . . . or, by taking our place among the comunity of nations, becoming the prosperous western outlet on the North Pacific of a young and vigorous people, the eastern boundary of whose possessions is washed by the Atlantic.[33]

Despite his legal and political successes, Crease, it would seem, also made enemies, the most notable being Amor de Cosmos, politician and fiery editor of the *Colonist*.

Through the years, de Cosmos was both for and against a number of political issues. When Crease won his first election, de Cosmos was busy waging a tireless campaign against the Hudson's Bay Company, James Douglas, and anyone else he suspected of being company linked, including Henry Crease. His editorial in January 1860 had even intimated that "agents of the Company [had] secured the return of Tolmie and Crease" to power. De Cosmos's caustic and often bitingly poisonous pen continued to attack Henry Crease and his contemporaries in the newspapers of the day.

Sarah Lindley Crease joined her husband in late February 1860. Her arrival aboard the *Athelstan* was welcomed by Henry, but Sarah was surprised to find that her husband was already involved in the stormy political scene.

Sarah was the artistic elder daughter of a famous London botanist Dr. John Lindley. She was born in a suburb of London in November 1826, and grew up with a love of gardens and a wide knowledge of plant life, passed on by her father. She also was a proficient artist and enjoyed engraving on copper, sketching botanical specimens, and making watercolour sketches. She spoke both French and German and enjoyed reading and writing. Her mother's strong religious beliefs had been a large part of Sarah's life since childhood, and one of her earliest memories was being present at Queen Victoria's coronation in Westminster Abbey.

It was perhaps their mutual love of art that had first brought Henry Crease and Sarah Lindley together. Sarah once described her feelings for Henry in a typically Victorian manner:

> You know how I have told you before, that I fell in love with your drawings (the coloured ones in those days). I read in them a character which I was sure I could not help loving.[34]

The couple married at Acton Church in London on April 27, 1853, and Sarah sketched her own wedding cake, which stood two feet high with the ornaments. After a honeymoon on the Isle of Wight, the Creases settled in St. James Square in London. When Henry left to seek his fortune in the new world in 1858, Sarah waited at home with their daughters.

She set sail to join her husband in August 1859, and the voyage must have seemed like going to the very ends of the earth. It was a particularly brave thing to do, for she had always disliked the sea and was terrified by some of her unpleasant experiences during the six months before she reached Victoria.

Initial impressions of Victoria were not good. The family's first accommodation was in bare, cold rooms that they were forced to share with a family of rats. Later they secured a small cottage on Fort Street and eventually moved to Fernwood, the house that Crease's friend, Benjamin W. Pearse, had built. Pearse, being a bachelor at that time, had no need for such a large home. During her first months in Victoria, Sarah began painting watercolour sketches. Many of these she sent to her family back in England as a pictorial record of her early impressions so that they could better understand the life she was now leading. Making them was "a pleasure and a solace to the 'home sickness' that most people going to a far country know so well."[35]

Her father entered these sketches in the British Columbia Department of Canada section of the London International Exhibition of 1862. According to Sarah's own inscription on the cover of one of the twelve paintings she sent home, she claims that her father's "sole object in displaying these poor sketches to the public, was simply for the interest of those who had dear friends or relatives in Victoria, BC, and for those who might be thinking of going to that Colony themselves."[36]

Like Joseph Pemberton's books, Sarah Crease's watercolours served as a descriptive record of life in the young colony. She sketched the fort in its last days, the red-brick government buildings, Government, Yates, and Fort streets, Native women, churches, and pretty landscape scenes.

Late in 1861, the Creases moved to New Westminster, which was quickly overtaking Victoria as a social and political centre. Henry Crease had been made Attorney General of BC by then, and his work was chiefly centred on the mainland.

Before long, the Creases were part of that close-knit circle of upper-class families whose social life was extremely full. In her book, *A Pioneer Gentlewoman in British Columbia*, Susan Allison wrote of this social life:

> We met many friends, Judge Crease and his family, our old friend, Mr. O'Reilly and his wife, formerly Miss Trutch (sister to Joe and John Trutch) . . . Our society leaders were Mrs. Trutch, Mrs. O'Reilly, Mrs. Crease.[37]

Perhaps it was this active time as "society leaders" in New Westminster that set the pace for these ladies to form the social nucleus in Victoria over the next four decades. Their New Westminster social activities at Government House or aboard ships such as the *Cameleon* and the *Sparrowhawk* meant "lots of gaiety for the young people."[38]

Colonel Moody and the Royal Engineers organized theatricals, dances, and musical events. Picnics were held along the banks of the Fraser River in summer and skating parties in winter. During this period, the Creases also attended the opening of the Alexandra Suspension Bridge with their friends, the Trutches.

Their home on Sapperton Road was called Ince Cottage, and during their years in New Westminster, two more children were born to them, Josephine and Lindley. The Trutches were godparents to Josephine.

From 1861 until 1870, Henry Crease drafted most of the laws for the new colony, so his role in the settlement and establishment of the area was quite considerable. He described this time rather amusingly:

> Became Attorney General in July, 1861. Worked like blazes and did all the Government business in the House and drew and fought thro' the House over 500 Acts of Parliament & the Crown business of Colony.[39]

In 1868, the Creases, with their five children, moved back to Victoria where the new capital of the joint colonies was finally to be established. They had made many investments on the mainland, so the move back to Vancouver Island was not financially satisfactory.

Their first task was to find a suitable home for their growing family; two more sons were born to them, Henry and Arthur. For a while the Creases rented Woodlands on Government Street near Beacon Hill Park, the home of James Bissett. In October 1871, they picked a property on Fort Street Hill (the part that was then known as Cadboro Bay Road), which belonged to Edward Graham Alston. It consisted of five acres of fields and oak trees, and an old house they planned to remodel. A few days before they were due to move in, the house mysteriously burned to the ground, so again the family was temporarily homeless and financially harmed.

They found a house to rent at the corner of Menzies and Superior streets but still owned the Alston land and, in 1874, they laid the cornerstone for their own home on that acreage. The new house, completed in 1875, was called Pentrelew, a Cornish word meaning "house-on-land-sloping-two-ways," and was later to become important in the province as a political and social centre.

There were eventually six Crease children growing up at Pentrelew. Son Henry had died in infancy and one daughter, Barbara, died young. Apart from these tragedies, the Crease home was a happy one. Sarah taught all four daughters to sketch and, as was to be expected, the two Crease sons became interested in law.

When Lindley and Arthur Crease were growing up, there was a notable lack of good boys' schools in Victoria, so Lindley was sent to England to be educated; he was only ten years old. He began his schooling at Conynghan House School in Ramsgate, where he was teased unmercifully about his Canadian background. Nicknamed "Beavergrease" or "Greasepot," he suffered these insults bravely as he attempted to settle into the strange English way of life.[40] Later, after excelling at sports and winning prizes for English and French, he was enrolled at Haileybury College. He returned to Canada in 1885. His brother, Arthur, who had attended the Boys' Collegiate School in Victoria, was also sent to Haileybury College in 1886 at age fourteen.[41]

The Crease girls received their education in Victoria, first from their mother at home, then at Mrs. Fellows' Private School for Girls, and later at Angela College on Burdett Street, where Henry Crease's sister, Emily Howard Crease, was principal in the 1870s, following in the footsteps of Susan Pemberton. Later, both Susan and Josephine Crease took art courses through the Ladies Department at King's College, London, a bold and innovative move for young women at that time. The entire Crease family, through their love of and dedication to art, were later very active in Victoria's art circles. Josephine Crease was particularly involved in the Victoria Sketch Club, which was formed in 1900, and in 1903 she was elected president.

The family was also very community minded. Anglican by religion and Conservative in their politics, various family members were also involved with the formation of the Alexandra Club, the Masonic Order, St. Andrew's Lodge, and the Men's Canadian Club. Sarah Crease was an accomplished and charming hostess, a little in advance of her time, as evidenced by her interest in women's rights movements. She was an active member of such organizations as the Local Council of Women and the Imperial Order of Daughters of the Empire. Her daughters, Susan and Josephine, were involved in similar issues. In recognition of her work with the Local Council of Women, Susan Crease was awarded the Queen's Silver Jubilee Medal in 1935. Josephine was a particularly active organizer of the Alexandra Rose Tag Days, which raised much-needed money for hospitals.

All these activities show that, despite their wealth and position in society, the Crease women were far from idle. Indeed, they used their power and influence to achieve a great deal for the community.

In the early years, Sarah Crease frequently accompanied her husband on the mainland when he carried out his judicial duties there, by steamer, stage coach, private coach, or simply on horseback. A brave woman, she endeavoured to keep pace with her husband at all times, witnessing first-hand the rough life of the Cariboo.

Following a horse-riding accident, Judge Crease was forced to hold court while lying on a stretcher in great pain. Sarah was there at his side, assisting as best she could. Another time, she witnessed her husband being held at gun-point when they were riding through wilderness. Her unusually calm reaction to this episode, which might have caused a more faint-hearted woman to experience an attack of the vapours, probably prevented a tragedy, and the incident passed off without harm.

Even at home, life was not without its excitement. In March 1887, Ah Chu, a Chinese servant, who had previously been a loyal, hard worker, suddenly seized an oil can and threw it on the kitchen fire, spreading flames across the floor and into the nearby wood box. Obviously deranged, he then grabbed a large kitchen knife and proceeded to attack a guest staying at Pentrelew, who had tried to calm him. The guest received numerous wounds before the servant fled, by which time everyone was more concerned with trying to extinguish the fire. A contractor working on a nearby building ran to Pentrelew with his men and, with the aid of a hose, finally managed to quell the flames.

Meanwhile, the servant had taken off for Clover Point, and there he attempted to end his life by rushing headlong into the water. A spectator dragged him to safety, and it was later discovered that he had swallowed a quantity of the coal oil himself prior to the incident.

The Chinese culture was obviously very foreign and, although having Chinese servants was customary among the elite of Victoria, families such as the Creases often found the Chinese difficult to get along with and made little or no attempt to understand them. Many misunderstandings occurred as a result of differences in language and customs.

A rather patronizing letter written by Sarah Crease in 1864 illustrates this attitude of many upper-class families to their Chinese servants:

> We have all been longing to let you know what a charming Chinaman we have got. I don't know when we have had things so comfortable as since he came. He is clean, orderly and industrious, bakes and cooks to our hearts content . . . God, I'm sure, sends such Chinamen as all good things come from Him.[42]

In 1896, a great honour was bestowed upon Henry Crease; a memo was received from Lord Aberdeen on January 1:

> It gives me much pleasure to inform you that the Queen approves of the bestowal of Knighthood upon you on the occasion of your retirement from an honorable judicial career, commencing so many years ago, that you are now the only remaining Judge in Canada appointed directly by the Imperial Government. Accept sincere congratulations and best wishes.[43]

The judge was now to be known as the Honourable Sir Henry Pering Pellew Crease. The *Colonist* of January 3, 1896, was ecstatic in its praise, this being one year after the death of Amor de Cosmos, a Crease critic, and long after his association with that newspaper. The paper reported:

> The people of British Columbia will be well satisfied the Queen has been pleased to confer the honour of knighthood upon Mr. Justice Crease. They will, no doubt, look upon it as a fitting closing of a useful and honorable career at the bar and upon the bench. The new Knight's ability as a Judge has gained for him the respect of British Columbians generally and his uniform courtesy, his geniality and his amiability secured for him hosts of friends, in every part of the province. Sir Henry carries with him into

retirement the esteem and good wishes of all who have had the privilege of making his acquaintance in any capacity.[44]

Sir Henry lived on for nine more years at Pentrelew until his death there in 1905. Lady Crease outlived him by many years, dying in 1922 at ninety-six.

Following Sarah Crease's death, Lindley, Josephine, and Susan continued to live at Pentrelew, attempting to uphold the old traditions and the style of social life that had once existed there.

Mary Maberly Crease was the only daughter to marry. She and an English lawyer, Frederick George Walker, were wed in 1886 and had five children: Madge, Jerry, twins Freda and Joan, and Harvey.

Though Lindley Crease never married, he was engaged twice. In 1903, his brother Arthur married Helen Louise Tyrwhitt-Drake, a childhood friend of the Crease children, and the daughter of another judge. The couple had four children: Harry, Maude, Thomas, and John.

The name of Crease has survived in Victoria through the law firm of Crease & Company. Established in 1891 by Lindley Crease (who had been admitted to the Bar in 1890), the firm later included his brother, Arthur, and Frederick C. Fowkes. Through the years since then, there have been many legal connections to the original firm, but eventual amalgamation of all these legal lineages became the law firm of Crease & Company. A further reorganization and amalgamation with Harman & Company in 1992 created the firm of Crease, Harman & Company.

Many of the Crease family are buried in Ross Bay Cemetery in Victoria. Arthur, the youngest of Sarah and Henry Crease's children and the last remaining Crease of the original legal dynasty, died in 1967.

The Crease family had greatly influenced the social life and times of early Victoria, just as the name Crease still pulls considerable weight in legal circles well over a century later.

# The O'Reilly Family

O'Reilly siblings. Left to right: Charlotte Kathleen O'Reilly, Francis
Joseph O'Reilly, and Arthur John O'Reilly. Date: undetermined.
IMAGE C-3939 COURTESY OF ROYAL BC MUSEUM, BC ARCHIVES

Mr. Commissioner O'Reilly . . . fully confirms the previous reports of successful mining in winter at Cariboo. He adds "Labour is in great demand at rates varying from $10 to $12 per diem."

—Douglas to Colonial Secretary the
Duke of Newcastle, May 18, 1863

Peter O'Reilly was meticulous about keeping up his diary entries, rarely neglecting his daily writings, however busy were his days.

The summer of 1886 had been especially busy for the O'Reilly family, the highlight being the visit of Sir John and Lady Macdonald. The prime minister and his wife arrived in Victoria in late July and thereafter kept up a social whirl of activity with the elite of Victoria for several weeks. It had meant attendance at many social occasions for the O'Reillys, but they gladly embraced the chance to entertain and be entertained by their counterparts at balls, dinners, and luncheons.

Peter continued to keep a daily record of events. He noted the garden party at Government House, a dance at the Dunsmuirs', a dinner at Armadale, a ball at the Assembly Hall, and of course, the O'Reillys' own luncheon, high tea, and extravagant torchlight regatta along the Selkirk waters. His wife, Carry, and daughter, Puss (his nickname for Kathleen), had also spent a great deal of time in the company of Lady Macdonald on frequent drives around Victoria.

But now, as Peter penned yet another diary entry at his desk, he thought back to when he had called at the Driard Hotel to meet with Sir John for a "long chat." Their meeting had been cordial and they covered much ground, but one thing had particularly amused Peter O'Reilly.

Macdonald's secretary, Joseph Pope, stated that the Driard Hotel was over-charging the prime minister and his party for their stay there. The somewhat exorbitant amounts were brought to the attention of Sir John who, despite his well-known economical views and often parsimonious ways, had simply replied that "Of course the bills have to be paid!" The reply again caused Peter to chuckle.

The prime minister's visit was now drawing to a close. The following day, August 13, Sir John would formally open the Esquimalt & Nanaimo Railway at Cliffside, near Shawnigan Lake. Many of Peter O'Reilly's contemporaries would journey in the party to witness that historic event.

It would be the realization and fulfilment of many long-anticipated dreams for Victoria and the west. He felt proud to be a part of it.

# CHAPTER FIVE

# *In a Whirl of High Society*

I t has long been believed that most of the old-country traditions established in the colony in the early years were introduced by the English or the Scots. The Irish element, however, was also strongly represented. They were equally loyal to queen and country, and equally intent upon preserving the style of life they had enjoyed at home.

The first Irishman to reside permanently on Vancouver Island was Joseph Despard Pemberton. He was followed by many others, among them Peter O'Reilly.

O'Reilly was born in 1828, the son of Patrick O'Reilly of Ballybeg House, County Meath, and Mary Blundell of Ince Hall, Lancashire. The O'Reillys and the Blundells were staunch Catholics but, in later life, Peter showed a distinct independence of character when he decided, just prior to leaving Ireland for Canada, to forsake the Roman Catholic Church and become a Protestant. Undoubtedly his decision came as a shock to his family. He kept it to himself, however, rather than use it to gain favour with the strong element of Protestant gentry in the young colony to which he was heading.

O'Reilly, who had received his education in Ireland, had spent seven years as an officer with the Irish Revenue Police (later known as the Royal Irish Constabulary). At the age of thirty, he decided to leave his homeland and try his luck in the new world.

He arrived in 1859 with a letter of introduction to James Douglas and, in April, he was offered an appointment as justice of the peace and stipendiary magistrate for the District of Langley. Later that same year, he took over the District of Fort Hope with responsibility also for Similkameen and Rock Creek until May 1862.

In subsequent years, O'Reilly's career skyrocketed. He served as magistrate and gold commissioner in the Cariboo, Kootenay-Columbia, and Omineca, and was appointed to the legislative council of British Columbia in 1863, where he served until 1871. In 1881, he was offered the prestigious position of Indian Reserve Commissioner for British Columbia.

In a confidential report on his officers, Douglas once described O'Reilly as "a gentleman of excellent character, high moral worth, an able, active resolute Magistrate," so O'Reilly was highly thought of and a definite asset to the colony.[45] It is interesting to discover, however, that early in his career he had a run-in with Captain William Moore, a well-known Fraser River steamboat captain. Captain Moore obviously did not think highly of O'Reilly, as can be seen from a letter he wrote to the editor of the *Colonist*:

> We have up here one O'Rilley [*sic*] . . . a justice of the peace—who holds the law in the palm of his hand. Some days ago I ordered one of my men to open a barrel of pork for the boat's use—which pork belongs to the boat's stores. The said O'Rilley ordered the pork to be seized. The next day he acknowledged that he had no right to seize the pork, but fined me $40 and one of my men $20. Upon asking him what the fine was for he refused to make any explanation. I am, therefore, led to believe that this is a new style instituted by the said O'Rilley for raising the wind.[46]

In general, O'Reilly seemed to be popular with the miners, managing to keep the peace and have his position of authority recognized and respected.

Maybe his initial announcement upon arrival in the Kootenay area helped him to gain this respect; it had certainly dispelled any problems from potential trouble-makers. He apparently said, "Now, boys, there must be no shooting, for if there is shooting, there will surely be hanging."[47]

In those early years, O'Reilly spent much of his time on the mainland, but he did manage to make occasional visits to Victoria and was often a dinner guest at Fairfield House, the home of the Trutch family. He had known Joseph Trutch for some time. Trutch had also arrived in the colony in 1859, and had spent time surveying the rural lands of the lower Fraser River, where the two men had first become acquainted.

It was at one of the Trutch dinner parties in Victoria that Peter O'Reilly met Joseph's sister, Caroline, who was visiting the colony from England, with her mother. Caroline had already heard of the handsome Peter O'Reilly from his exploits on the mainland, but this was the first occasion at which she had been introduced to him. It was love at first sight for both.

Caroline was the youngest child of William Trutch and Charlotte Barnes. She was exceptionally bright, having learned to read at the age of four, and she excelled at music. She also had a great love for the outdoors and enjoyed horseback riding.

Caroline's life had been far from ordinary up until her meeting with Peter O'Reilly. She was widely travelled and had already sampled life in many parts of the world. On one occasion she had visited a married sister in Madras, India, and en route had stopped in Egypt and Malta. She had especially liked the gaiety of life in India under the Raj, and her beautiful singing voice had been in great demand at many social events. Although she had revelled in the elegant balls and the exciting and colourful entertainment, Caroline had also been witness to numerous atrocities during the Sepoy Mutiny, an uprising of Indian troops against their British masters.

After Caroline left India, she travelled through Europe and returned briefly to England to stay with her mother shortly after her father's death. She then decided to accompany her mother to Vancouver Island from where, in 1860, her brother Joseph had written such glowing reports. "Come and make your home with us. There is no more trouble in coming out here than you had in going to Madras."[48]

However, for Caroline, adventure was paramount, so even their journey to Victoria had proved eventful. They visited St. Thomas in the West Indies and crossed the Isthmus of Panama in scorching temperatures. As they steamed into the Gulf of California, the sight of fleeing refugees had merely emphasized the tragedy taking place in the United States. It was late 1861 and the American Civil War would soon be in its second year.

Following the dinner party where Caroline and Peter met, they continued a courtship that ultimately led to their marriage on December 15, 1863. Their wedding day was picturesque, a brilliantly beautiful sunny morning shining on a sparkling world of recently fallen snow. Caroline was given away by her brother, and the ceremony, attended by many, took place in Christ Church Cathedral. A wedding breakfast was held at Fairfield House, followed by a honeymoon in Esquimalt.

The following spring, Peter returned to his duties in the Cariboo, and Caroline stayed with her mother in Victoria. Later, Peter and Caroline lived in New Westminster, and their first son was born there in 1866. The O'Reillys' social calendar in those early years was full, and possibly a preview of their later years in Victoria. As mentioned in *The Recollections of Susan Allison*, Caroline O'Reilly was one of the society leaders in New Westminster during that time period.

Some of the O'Reilly summers were spent at Yale on the Fraser River while winters were whiled away in Victoria. The O'Reillys now dwelt on an arm of Victoria harbour, at Point Ellice. Three more children (two daughters and a son) were born to them at Point Ellice House, which still stands today, one of the last homes remaining from those colonial days.

Captain Robert Scott, RN, taken at Esquimalt in 1891
(one of many of Kathleen O'Reilly's suitors).
IMAGE C-03906 COURTESY OF ROYAL BC MUSEUM, BC ARCHIVES.

Caroline's experiences travelling the globe were a great asset to her when she became Mrs. Peter O'Reilly. As the wife of a gold commissioner, she sometimes accompanied her husband to the interior, enjoying the outdoor life. Even before her marriage, she had taken part in mainland events, not the least of which had been the official opening in the fall of 1863 of the Alexandra Suspension Bridge, for which her brothers, John and Joseph Trutch, were largely responsible.

A loving husband, a devoted family, and a whirl of high-society life were now part of Caroline's agenda. However, her life was also not without tragedy. In 1876, she experienced the double trauma of the deaths of both her seven-year-old daughter, Amy, and her mother. Point Ellice House became a house of mourning.

Like most upper-class families, the O'Reillys sent their children to England to be educated but, being devoted parents, Peter and Caroline travelled back and forth on several occasions to visit their offspring. Kathleen grew into a young woman of considerable beauty. Following their education abroad, the three children returned to their home and became a part of the social scene in Victoria.

During the 1880s, Point Ellice House was at the centre of much social activity, with winter skating parties, summer picnics, riding, boating, lawn tennis, and cricket. The O'Reillys' lawn, which curved down to the banks of the harbour, was the scene of the first lawn tennis tournament in Victoria.

The yearly Gorge regattas on Queen Victoria's birthday were times of open house at Point Ellice. Naval personnel were frequently entertained there, as were the influential and important members of Victoria society. Not only had one of Caroline O'Reilly's brothers, Joseph, held the position of BC's first lieutenant-governor from 1871 to 1876, but her other brother, John, had married the sister of Anthony Musgrave, one-time governor of the colony. The families were therefore well ensconced in the high society of the day. Perhaps the highlight of the O'Reillys' social life was when they had Prime Minister Sir John A. Macdonald and his wife to dinner in 1886.

In February 1897, Kathleen was formally presented at court in Ireland to Queen Victoria's representative, His Excellency Lord Cudogan. This event was another crowning achievement for any socially inclined colonial family in those days. Needless to say, beautiful Kathleen was much sought after. Her numerous beaux included a young naval officer named Robert Scott, who later became famous for his tragically unsuccessful race against Norwegian Roald Amundsen to the South Pole. While he was stationed at

its original charming setting. Peter O'Reilly purchased Point Ellice House, built in 1861, for the sum of fourteen thousand dollars from Charles W. Wallace in 1868. As his family grew, O'Reilly added to and improved the original home, turning it into the house it is today. The last additions were dated 1889.

The house has witnessed many changes as industries have gradually encroached upon that once-elite residential area. Through it all, the O'Reilly family proudly refused to be forced out of their original acreage.

Point Ellice House is now owned by the provincial government, after over a century of being family owned, and is open to the public. It remains as a monument to that bygone era, a reminder that the Gorge was one of the most fashionable areas in Victoria.

Walking in the O'Reilly garden today is rather like taking a step back in time. There, among the curving brick and gravel paths, with the sweet aromas of spring lilac or summer jasmine in the air, one momentarily forgets that many decades have come and gone since Caroline O'Reilly herself strolled those paths with her husband and planned their garden. It could quite easily still be a hundred years ago. A boatload of visitors could be disembarking at the boathouse, about to stroll up the rolling green lawn to attend a croquet or tennis party and later to be entertained to tea.

The O'Reillys brought a certain distinction and a definite style to the upper-class social scene of early Victoria. Peter's original family connections in Ireland, his marriage into the Trutch family, their political, governmental, and naval connections, and being a part of social events such as a court presentation set them a little apart from the others in terms of grandeur and importance.

They added a touch of icing to the aristocratic cake.

# The Trutch Family

Trutches and O'Reillys, taken on steps of Fairfield House.
Left to right: Joseph Trutch, Caroline O'Reilly (Kathleen on knee),
Julia Trutch (standing), old Mrs. Trutch (seated), young Frank
O'Reilly and John Trutch (on steps).
IMAGE D-03510 COURTESY OF ROYAL BC MUSEUM, BC ARCHIVES

You may rest assured that [BC] will not regard this railway engagement as a
"cast-iron contract," as it has been called, or desire that it should be carried
out in any other way than will secure the prosperity of the whole Dominion
of which she is a part.

—Joseph Trutch, April 1871

Joseph Trutch was in eastern Canada when news reached him that he was to be British Columbia's first lieutenant-governor.

He had, of course, been in Ottawa on many occasions in the year leading up to Confederation; it seemed that his life had been forever devoted to that cause alone. His dream had always been for a Canada united from ocean to ocean, so he believed that Confederation was the only course to take, the only option for true Canadians.

The thought of annexation with the United States was deplorable to him. He had never liked Americans, despite having married one. His wife, Julia, was the one exception to his rule about "uncouth and vulgar" Americans. She was cultured and well-bred, almost English in her outlook. Very often he even forgot that she had been born in America.

So, in July 1871, when BC finally joined Confederation, Trutch was particularly proud of the successful conclusion to all his hard work, and his appointment as lieutenant-governor was an honour he gladly accepted.

The journey back to take up his new post was long and arduous. He travelled via San Francisco where he boarded HMS *Sparrowhawk* and then endured a further ten days of boisterous seas before finally reaching Victoria on August 15. But it had given him ample time to think about the past and contemplate his future. He knew he had numerous political enemies, those who assumed his appointment was one of patronage. He vowed he would prove himself to those who doubted his abilities. He would serve his time and work hard for the good of the province.

The new lieutenant-governor and his wife were driven first to Fairfield House, their previous home. There they took up temporary residence until they moved into Cary Castle, which would become their official residence for the next five years.

It was a time of transition for BC, and Joseph and Julia Trutch, a successful blend of stuffy British formality and fresh American freedom, would prove to be excellent first caretakers of Victoria's Government House.

CHAPTER SIX

# The Terms, the Whole Terms, and Nothing But the Terms

The story of the Trutch family in British Columbia has always been intertwined with that of the O'Reillys. Apart from their relationship through marriage, they also became two of the most prominent families in early Victoria's high society.

The Trutch story begins in the West Indies in November 1799, where a daughter, Charlotte, was born to the Honourable Joseph Barnes and his wife, the former Hannah Williams. Joseph Barnes was already well established in the county of Somerset in England, but he also owned considerable property in the West Indies and was at that time a member of the legislative council of Jamaica. He was a man of considerable wealth, as well as an assistant judge of the Supreme Court, and for twenty years he was the mayor of Kingston.

Charlotte was a bright child and at an early age was sent back to London to further her education. Every year her mother would faithfully sail from the West Indies to England to visit her. Meanwhile, Charlotte became proficient at her studies as well as at the piano and harp, and her soprano voice was a delight to all who heard her.

On her sixteenth birthday Charlotte attended her first ball, and there she met William Trutch. Seven years later, in 1822, they were married.

William Trutch was a solicitor by profession and something of an adventurer by nature. After his marriage he took his bride back to the West Indies, where he accepted a position as clerk of the peace in St. Thomas.

The young Trutches made their home in Jamaica until 1834 and then returned to England, where William resumed his career in law. Their marriage produced five children: two sons, Joseph and John, and three daughters, Caroline, Charlotte, and Emily. The boys, who were only two years apart in age, both attended Mount Radford School in Exeter.

Joseph had early inclinations toward engineering and at seventeen was apprenticed to the engineering firm of John Rennie. He stayed there for five years, during which time he worked on the construction of the Great Western Railway. Like many of his contemporaries, Joseph was also always looking for adventure and a way to become rich.

News of the California gold rush in 1849 excited him, despite his typically British aversion to gold fever as such. He could, however, see numerous ways in which money might be made as a result of a gold rush, so, on July 18 that year, he left Gravesend in England aboard the *Favourite*, sailed across the Atlantic, rounded the Horn, and headed for San Francisco. He arrived there in January 1850, having made a brief stop in Chile where, he later remarked, he had been treated with the respect he thought he, as an Englishman, deserved. Upon his arrival in San Francisco, Trutch was in for a severe case of culture shock. His obvious dislike of the country and its inhabitants became more and more apparent in his letters home. To his sister Emily he wrote, in April 1850, that the city of San Francisco, was a haven for "unsuppressed vice and iniquity of every shape that the world has realized." He thought that Americans in general were bad-mannered and vulgar, and their swearing was beyond belief—"the most revolting and blasphemous oaths are quite common in conservation."[51] He firmly believed that Americans were untrustworthy and never spoke the truth, and admitted to his father that he was "quite out of his element among such people."

This last statement was, of course, undoubtedly true, and Americans probably found this rather pompous Englishman equally strange. It should be pointed out that Joseph Trutch was the product of a totally Victorian and very respectable English environment, composed of a class of ladies and gentlemen who considered themselves to be superior in every way. Nevertheless, despite a dislike of what he described as "those vulgar Americans," he did manage to conduct some profitable business deals in San Francisco. He later admitted that he regretted not having met any "capitalists" in San Francisco with whom he might have entered into even better business arrangements.

By the end of May, Trutch had left San Francisco and was on his way to Oregon in the company of a Captain Keyes of the US Artillery. There, he found life a little more to his liking. He appreciated and enjoyed the quiet, undeveloped countryside where there were opportunities to hunt and fish, and where he also found friendly people eager and willing to cater to him in the style that he thought he deserved.

He worked on the survey and building of the town of St. Helens, and by July 1851 was also surveying and laying out the town of Milton. He then spent some time surveying the Puget Sound area and the mouth of the Columbia River. By the summer of 1852, he had received an appointment as assistant surveyor to John Bower Preston, the first United States surveyor general in that territory.

Joseph's brother, John, had also come out from England by this time, so the two men were able to work together on many joint projects for the surveyor general. Before long, the Trutch brothers had become well entrenched in the Oregon social scene, especially through their connection with the Preston family. It was at one of the Preston family gatherings that Joseph met Mrs. Preston's sister, Julia Hyde, who was living with them.

Julia and Joseph had much in common, despite her American heritage. She was a cultivated, highly intelligent woman who, like Joseph, enjoyed the finer things in life. She could talk knowledgeably about music and literature and, like him, found the pioneer life somewhat disagreeable.

They were immediately attracted to one another and were married in January 1855 in Oregon City. Soon afterward, they moved to Michigan to an even more civilized way of life. Later, on a visit to England, Joseph and his wife met Lieutenant-Colonel R.C. Moody of the Royal Engineers, who was about to leave for BC.

Meanwhile, in 1857, John Trutch had also left Oregon and had moved to Vancouver Island. When Moody suggested to Joseph in London that he too should consider a move to BC so that he would still be living under the Crown but in an environment of great opportunity, it seemed like an excellent idea.

Joseph and Julia Trutch arrived on Vancouver Island in June 1859. On the recommendation of Colonel Moody, Joseph received a contract from Governor Douglas to survey some rural lands of BC. There was a slight dispute over the initial contract, which stated that Trutch would have preferential treatment over others in future contracts. Douglas would not agree to this clause, so Joseph threatened to sue him for going back on his word. Finally, a completely new contract was drawn up, ensuring that Trutch would be paid ten thousand dollars for his services. This contract seemed to appease all the parties concerned.

Within three months Trutch had completed his work, with which Douglas was delighted, and had received other government contracts for more work. Between 1860 and 1863, he completed contracts for the laying out of the Harrison-Lillooet Road and the famous Cariboo Road itself from Yale to Lytton.

This was merely the beginning for Joseph Trutch. In 1863 he was again associated with his brother, John, on the construction of the Alexandra Suspension Bridge across the Fraser River at Spuzzum. It was the first such suspension bridge in British North America and was a major triumph for the Trutch brothers. In addition, Joseph gradually became embroiled in the political scene of BC, being elected to the legislative council of Vancouver Island in November 1861. A year after the completion of the suspension bridge, he was appointed chief commissioner of lands and works for BC. This government appointment resulted in a major conflict of interest. It was felt that Trutch held too many personal stakes in the province to have a government position as well. His interests by this time ranged from ownership and, therefore, collection of tolls on the Alexandra and the Thompson River bridges, to numerous land holdings on Vancouver Island. In all, he apparently had "a direct interest in Colonial works to the value of $97,500.00."[52]

The conflict of interest was resolved by Trutch agreeing to dispose of most of his holdings, although he was unable to sell the Alexandra Bridge because the price he was asking for it (thirty thousand dollars) was far out of reach of any private individual and the government itself refused to buy it. The Trutch brothers were, therefore, forced to retain their interest. Nevertheless, Joseph did decide to accept the government position as chief commissioner of lands and works. Needless to say, he was now a very wealthy man.

During the following years, he also proved himself to be a man of integrity and great ability. His new position gave him access to the executive and legislative councils of the colony. His initial upset with Governor Douglas had by then turned into a firm friendship, and the two men had great respect for one another. Trutch's other friends included Attorney General Henry Crease, his old friend from their Mount Radford school days, and future Governors Seymour and Musgrave, who later became his allies and close companions. It was in fact Trutch who brought Governor Seymour's body back to Victoria following the governor's death aboard HMS *Sparrowhawk* in June 1869.

The Trutch position in society was further cemented by the marriage of John Trutch to Governor Musgrave's sister, Zoe, in December 1870. Their sister, Caroline Trutch, had by this time married a gold commissioner, Peter O'Reilly, "thereby further consolidating Trutch's relationship with the establishment."[53]

Meanwhile, Confederation was the big issue of the day in political circles. Joseph Trutch had previously been less than enthusiastic toward the idea, but gradually he came to see the sense of it. There appeared to be no alternative, for he was adamantly opposed to any annexation arrangement with the United States. Following the debate and the passing in 1870 of the resolution that favoured union, Trutch, J.S. Helmcken, and Dr. R.W.W. Carrall were chosen to travel to Ottawa to negotiate for BC.

During those Ottawa negotiations, it was Trutch who suggested that the railway situation should be of prime importance in the terms, but he wanted this "railway engagement" to be included and carried out in a way that would "secure the prosperity of the whole Dominion of which she [BC] is a part."[54] Things seemed to be going well and other terms were quickly agreed upon, Trutch and his colleagues doing an admirable job. "He ... [Trutch] was everything and everybody," observed Helmcken, on one occasion.[55]

Once union seemed inevitable and the various terms safely settled, Trutch and his wife made more trips back to England. Joseph was basically still an Englishman at heart, and he much preferred the correct and proper lifestyle of his Victorian English background to that of the young colony of which he had by now become a very important part.

In Victoria, he and Julia enlarged their original "cottage" home to become the elegant Fairfield House. It stood on ten acres of land and soon became an important social centre, with its spacious rooms and elegant grounds.

Joseph Trutch had proved himself most impressive throughout the negotiations in Ottawa, and his astute, businesslike approach had certainly not gone unnoticed by Sir John A. Macdonald, Canada's prime minister.

Trutch was, therefore, considered to be the obvious choice for BC's first lieutenant-governor. In July 1871, he accepted this office in Ottawa and took the official oath in BC on August 14.

One of Trutch's first public appearances as BC's lieutenant-governor was to lay the cornerstone for St. Ann's convent school, the central portion of St. Ann's Academy in Victoria.

The first session of BC's provincial parliament was opened by Trutch in February 1872, with John F. McCreight as first premier. Peter O'Reilly noted after his brother-in-law's speech from the throne that "he [Joe] had acquitted himself with credit."[56] While McCreight remained as premier, Joseph Trutch played an equally important role in government affairs in the new province, but things changed once Amor de Cosmos formed the next administration in December 1872. The period of transition was over, and the Government of BC was well on its way to a more independent role, unencumbered by the old rules of colonial government days. Trutch had played a vital role in that all-important time of change.

Meanwhile, Julia Trutch enjoyed her role as the wife of the lieutenant-governor of BC. The Trutches left Fairfield House soon after Joseph's appointment and moved into Government House, then known as Cary Castle. There, Julia became the supreme example of the perfect hostess. She loved to entertain and delighted in both formal and informal occasions. Like her husband, she enjoyed the manners and customs of the old world. While sentries dressed in scarlet tunics guarded the gates of Cary Castle, Julia charmed her guests with dinner parties and balls inside its gracious walls. Christmastime was always very special for Julia. Despite her sorrow at having no children of her own, she loved to be surrounded by those of other people. She organized all the Christmas decorating with evergreens and candles galore, and chose the presents for her nieces and nephews with care and thought. Family prayers were encouraged and musical evenings were paramount.

After de Cosmos left office, the next premier to serve under Joseph Trutch was George Walkem, who held that office for two years. He was followed by Andrew C. Elliott. By that time, Trutch was himself growing somewhat bored with his position of "distinction and honour."[57] He confided to his brother-in-law, Peter O'Reilly, that he craved something more active. He was after all still a relatively young man.

On July 28, 1876, he made his decision to end his term as lieutenant-governor, and soon afterward he and Julia again left for England. In May of the following year, the Queen's Birthday Honours List announced that Joseph Trutch had been made a Companion of the Order of St. Michael & St. George, and later he became a Knight Commander. As Sir Joseph Trutch, his valuable services to his country had been rewarded royally. Sir Joseph and Lady Trutch returned to Fairfield House for a while to enjoy their new status. They also made more visits to England, where in many ways they were happier. They loved to travel, dividing their time among many countries and collecting rare art and valuable treasures.

Before long, however, the railway question was brewing once again, and Trutch knew instinctively that his services would be needed in BC to ensure that all the original terms of union were adhered to. For the sake of BC's future, which he feared might be in jeopardy, he felt he should be involved in the delicate negotiations about to take place.

Fortunately, his fears were unfounded, and Victoria and Ottawa were able to agree on all the proposals. Then, in February 1880, with the Conservatives back in power in Ottawa, Trutch's old friend John A. Macdonald decided to reward Trutch for his long service with a prestigious appointment as BC's confidential adviser to the Dominion government. As such, he would be dealing with public lands and the numerous complications that came about once the actual construction of the transcontinental railway began. Finally, it was a position to his liking and one into which he could really sink his teeth.

He retired nine years later at the age of sixty-three. Again, he and Julia left Fairfield House and returned to England, but when Julia became ill there, she craved to be back in Victoria where she believed her health would improve. "I was always well and happy there," she claimed.

The Trutches returned to Victoria full of optimism, but an improvement in Julia's health was not to be. She died the following July, in 1895. Her obituary in the *Colonist* summed up her importance in early Victoria's high-society life:

> She became one of the best appreciated society leaders of the capital, and when her husband received the appointment of Lieutenant-Governor, she presided at Government House with a dignity and, at the same time, affability which admirably befitted her position. In her private life, Lady Trutch was generous, but unostentatious.[58]

Her many acts of special kindness included Sunday school work, being involved with Agnes Weston's temperance work among sailors of the British navy, and involvement with numerous charities. She was a very talented artist and musician, and liked to be surrounded by things of beauty.

Left on his own, Joseph Trutch became a lonely, desperately sad man. Soon after Julia's death, he returned to England one last time and spent the remaining years of his retirement, until his death in March 1904, in Taunton, Somerset, at his home, Harton Manor.

Both Joseph and John Trutch were legends in BC's history. Men of honour and distinction, they were also in many ways products of their time. Joseph was considered by many to be a typical stuffy Englishman. His early engineering appointments in the province were probably earned because of his reliability as a man of integrity rather than his possession of any special abilities. Likewise, his later rise to great political heights may have been due to his knack of infiltrating the right circles with his gentlemanly manner, and by having the necessary important connections. In that respect, his West Indies background had also proved valuable. Despite both business and family connections, he was nonetheless a most able engineer, an excellent politician, and an exceptional negotiator.

Joseph Trutch was also an enormous snob. Being a product of "imperial England's confidence in the superiority of her own civilization,"[59] he always considered other races, notably the local Native people, to be inferior. His dealings with them, and his Indian land policy in particular, left much to be desired. In many of his letters, he makes such bigoted statements as "I think they [the Indians] are the ugliest and laziest creatures I ever saw, and we shod. [should] as soon think of being afraid of our dogs as of them."[60]

It should, of course, be remembered that remarks such as these were quite common among early colonists, especially those who came from so-called suitable backgrounds in England. Joseph Trutch's opinions, and his constant referral to Native people as "savages," do reveal a different side to his otherwise impeccable character. It has been suggested that, largely because of his bigoted attitude, the Indian land question in BC in his day left a "legacy of litigation that in the long run was to cost the province more than extinguishing Indian title and laying out reasonable reserves would have done."[61]

Throughout the careers of both brothers, Joseph's achievements tended to override those of his brother, John. John was, however, an equally able engineer and received many important contracts in his early days in BC. By marrying Zoe Musgrave, he made his career and future success in the province even more secure.

John and Zoe Trutch lived on the mainland for many years but also spent time at Fairfield House. In 1885, John took a position with the Esquimalt & Nanaimo Railway and, in an 1888 directory, his address is given as 114 Humboldt Street, Victoria.

In 1890, John's occupation was listed as land commissioner and he and Zoe were living on Richardson Street in Victoria, sharing a telephone number with Fairfield House. The Trutch family was one of the first in Victoria to own a telephone. The telephone had, in fact, arrived in the city only ten years earlier, in 1880, when a line was opened between W.J. Jeffree's clothing store and Pendray's soap factory. Two years before that, the first telephone line in regular use in BC had been run between Wellington and the docks at Departure Bay, the brainchild of a coal mine mechanic by the name of William H. Wall. (This was quite a feat, considering that it was in March 1876 that Alexander Graham Bell had initiated the first transmission of human voice over wires in Brantford, Ontario.)

In 1892, John and Zoe left Victoria for England. Zoe died there soon afterward, but John lived on until 1907 and died at seventy-nine. Both the Trutch brothers had finally come home to rest in their beloved England.

With no Trutch descendants from the union of Joseph and Julia Trutch, the line continued through John and Zoe's daughter, Charlotte E. Kelly, who lived in the Nanaimo area until the 1950s. In the late 1950s, Mrs. Kelly and her son, Michael, of Ottershaw, Surrey, England, presented the University of British Columbia with a valuable collection of documents, mainly correspondence between the two Trutch brothers during their early years in BC.

This collection has helped historians piece together some important missing years in BC's history, and helps show that the Trutch family story is an important part of the social fabric of the province.

# The Rithet Family

Rithet children: Jack (standing), Edward (seated), and Gertrude.
IMAGE A-01737 COURTESY OF ROYAL BC MUSEUM, BC ARCHIVES

[Robert Rithet] . . . is a leading business man, a public spirited, useful and energetic citizen who, having made his money in this city, has invested it here. Under the circumstances of an increasing population and enlarged revenue the presence of a man like R.P. Rithet at the helm is indispensable. We hope he will consent to stand.

—*Colonist*, November 28, 1884, on
promoting Robert Rithet for mayor

When a man's only daughter is about to be married, he has every right to feel apprehensive.

Robert Rithet was no exception to this rule on the afternoon of July 16, 1904, when his daughter Gertrude was about to become the bride of Lawrence Arthur Genge, son of the Genges of Surrey, England.

Hollybank had never looked lovelier. The Rithets' home had been the scene of many memorable social occasions through the years, but this one was special and would, he felt sure, far outshine any of the others. The reception to be held there that evening would be delightful. His wife, Lizzie, was an outstanding hostess, and she never failed to amaze him with her abilities to make guests feel comfortable in their charming, elegant home. Today, as the mother of the bride, she would rise to the occasion once more.

As for himself, well, that was quite another matter. His beautiful Gertrude was to become a bride in a matter of minutes, and he must appear to be the proud papa, confident and secure in the knowledge that his daughter would be happy. He knew this to be true. Genge was a man of integrity and Gertrude had made a wise choice. But . . . he was still a father, with a father's natural concern. He wanted the best for his daughter. He wanted her to be happy. He would be mortified for her if things should go wrong.

Suddenly she appeared in the room before him, ready to be escorted to Christ Church Cathedral, radiant in a gown of white crepe de Chine, trimmed with duchess lace. She was surrounded by a mass of orange blossom, and she carried a bouquet of roses. In his eyes, she had never looked more beautiful.

He felt her hand tremble slightly as he took it in his, and for a moment he remembered when she was a little girl and had clung to him after a nightmare, asking him to tell her stories of his adventures until she fell asleep again. She had called him "dear Papa" then, just as she did now, but this time she was somehow comforting him and telling him not to worry about her. Everything would be all right, and she was going to be very happy with her new husband.

And then she linked her arm through his and together they left for the cathedral.

# CHAPTER SEVEN

# San Francisco in Miniature

In the beginning, it was the Hudson's Bay Company that largely influenced Victoria's social life. Later it was the colonists settling the land who led the way socially. As we have seen, some of these men came from influential backgrounds, while others were, for various reasons, simply considered to be suitable. They had all arrived with the intention of finding a better life.

Before the gold rushes of 1858 and 1862, life in the colony was reasonably quiet and pleasant, and certainly not particularly conducive to business and commerce. By the beginning of the 1860s, this situation began to change rapidly. A need grew for merchants, real estate investors, storekeepers, and speculators in general.

And Victoria was now playing host to a completely different type of settler, both adventurous and ambitious, out to seek his fortune and make his mark. Entrepreneurs were arriving and setting a new course for Victoria's development. Eventually they even infiltrated the all-powerful establishment. Where class and background had always played the most important role, suddenly money did. These entrepreneurs were making a great deal of it, and their money was doing the talking.

In effect, Victoria was slowly becoming a "San Francisco in miniature."[62] This new gold rush society proved to be very cosmopolitan, and, given Victoria's already strong commercial ties with San Francisco and the many Americans entering the colony, it was inevitable that this new breed of entrepreneur would also share in Victoria's expansion, success, and ultimately its social life.

Robert Paterson Rithet was one of the best examples of this new breed of settler and one of the first to secure a foothold in Victoria's commercial centre. The son of a farmer, he was born in April 1844, in Scotland. Before coming to British Columbia in 1862, he had tried his luck in Liverpool, working for a merchant, and then the lure of the Cariboo brought him to North America. He fully intended to join in the gold rush, but soon began to realize that more money could be made in the business of mining the miners than it could by mining the actual gold.

He began work in Victoria as a stevedore and was offered the position of bookkeeper for the wholesale provision firm of Sproat & Company. He was soon running the Victoria office, since owner Gilbert Sproat was often absent in London directing the Committee on the Affairs of British Columbia. By 1869, at age twenty-five, Rithet had proved himself worthy of a promotion and was sent to San Francisco to deal with the company's interests there.

While there, he made one of the most important business connections of his life, one that set him firmly on the road to commercial success. He was introduced to Gilbert Sproat's San Francisco partner, Andrew Welch, already a very wealthy and prominent member of the elite. Welch had business dealings in many areas, including some from the time he had spent working with Sproat in an Alberni sawmill. He later did much to develop the shipping trade between Victoria and San Francisco and, before his death in 1889, had become a multimillionaire. Young Robert Rithet learned a great deal from him.

On one of his many trips back to Victoria, Rithet had formed an alliance with a young lady whose mother strongly disapproved of his attentions. In a rather typical Victorian manner, Rithet decided to break off his engagement to her, and he did this by writing a formal letter to her mother in very proper and stilted terms:

Victoria, Vancouver Island. 16th April
Saturday.
Mrs. Sutton,
View Street.

Madam: Referring to the conversation I had with you yesterday morning, the leading points in which, in order to avoid any misunderstanding, I condense as follows:

1. You refused to allow Miss Sutton to keep an appointment to go out with me on that day (yesterday).

2. You informed me that it was your intention not to allow Miss Sutton to go out with me in future unless some other members of your family accompanied us.

3. You stated that you regretted Miss Sutton had formed an attachment for a gentleman who hated the other members of your family.

After careful consideration of the foregoing, of your general conduct toward me of late, and of the fact of Miss Sutton's acceding to your demands, thereby ignoring my position, I have come to the conclusion that to carry out the engagement existing between Miss Sutton and myself would result in nothing but unhappiness under such circumstances, and I have therefore decided that it would be more to the interest of all concerned that the engagement referred to should be cancelled, and I will from this time consider it so, and beg to request that you will intimate my decision to Miss Sutton.

Regretting the intimacy which has existed betwixt Miss Sutton and myself and wishing you and all members of your family every happiness.
I am, Madam,
      Your obedient servant,
      R.P. Rithet[63]

His decision to end the entanglement may have been for a reason other than merely taking heed of an angry mother's warning. He had already met and fallen in love with one of the three daughters of Alexander Munro, chief factor of the Hudson's Bay Company in Victoria. Young Elizabeth (Lizzie) Munro was tall, slender, and exceedingly beautiful, and from the moment Robert first laid eyes on her when she was sixteen, he was in love. They were eventually married on October 27, 1875, when Lizzie was twenty-two.

Rithet had left Sproat's company in 1870 to join forces with J. Robertson Stewart, another well-established British merchant in Victoria, and by May of the next year he was managing the business during Stewart's illness. When Stewart decided to sell his business and retire to Scotland, Andrew Welch, with Robert Rithet's strong backing, bought him out.[64]

Soon afterward, the newspapers announced a new firm under the name of Welch, Rithet & Company, successors of Robertson Stewart. At that time, Rithet wrote to his new partner, Andrew Welch:

> We began under very favourable auspices, when the colony seems to be about to enter an era of improvement and progress . . . and with houses in San Francisco and Liverpool we should be able to make a business, and our outside connections are also tip-top.[65]

Robert Rithet's fortunes were now definitely on the rise and, by the time of his marriage to Elizabeth Munro, he was already an established business-man in Victoria.

During the 1870s and 1880s, his importance continued to grow. With Welch, he became involved in the sugar trade with the Hawaiian Islands and soon controlled a number of plantations there. He also acted as agent for the Moodyville Sawmill on Burrard Inlet and quickly began import-ing groceries and liquor into BC. The wealth he was accumulating was not wasted. He began investing in mills, in the Albion Ironworks in Victoria, and in sealing, whaling, and farming endeavours. In fact, his business interests spread so rapidly and he was responsible for so many BC outlets in wholesale, insurance, lumber, shipping, and canning that it would have been difficult to keep pace with him.

When Andrew Welch died in 1888, Rithet not only purchased his half interest, but also renamed the company R.P. Rithet & Co. Ltd. He was by then one of the wealthiest businessmen in the Pacific Northwest.

Hawaii was an independent country with its own queen, and Robert Rithet acted as Hawaii's consul-general in Victoria. In addition, he became one of the foremost sugar importers in North America. When Canadian sugar tariff laws changed in 1891, allowing sugar to be imported from China at a considerably lower price, he took advantage of the situation.

This move became the forerunner of the "sugar war" that raged between Victoria and Vancouver for three years. Rithet was bitterly opposed to the Rogers sugar refinery being located in Vancouver and fought for one in Victoria, trying at the same time to put the Vancouver operation out of business. When his Chinese sugar (imported from Butterfield & Swire in Hong Kong) suffered a loss on the BC market, he tried to organize a price-fixing arrangement with Vancouver. He was turned down and later, when the newspapers began a smear campaign against Chinese sugar because, they claimed, smallpox germs were being carried by bugs found in it, the whole thing proved too much for Rithet. He decided it was no longer worth the fight, reluctantly gave in to the pressures, and began to concentrate on his other, more profitable business ventures.

These other ventures were legion, ranging from the construction of the Outer Wharf in James Bay in the 1890s, enabling ocean-going liners such as the CPR Empress ships to dock there, to insurance connections through-out the world. Rithet served as general agent for the Queens Insurance Company of America, and the National Fire Insurance of Hartford, and as marine insurance agent for the Standard Marine Insurance Company of Liverpool. He also held a major interest in the BC Cattle Company and, having a love of horses, maintained a large farming acreage in the Broadmead district of Victoria where he bred and developed champions. It is believed that the name Broadmead was that of a stallion that Rithet brought from Australia.

Rithet also became briefly involved with engineer Sandford Fleming who developed standard time in North America; the two men made an unsuccessful attempt to lay a telegraph cable across the Pacific. Their project was aborted when they were chased off a remote island near Hawaii by a United States ship.

Despite all his many and varied business interests, Robert Rithet found time to enter politics. In November 1884, he put himself forward as a candidate for mayor of Victoria, and an editorial in the *Colonist* supported him strongly:

> For the position of mayor we know of no citizen who is better qualified to discharge the duties honestly and well than Mr. R.P. Rithet. He is a leading business man, a public spirited, useful and energetic citizen who, having made his money in this city, has invested it here. Under the circumstances of an increasing population and enlarged revenue the presence of a man like R.P. Rithet at the helm is indispensable. We hope he will consent to stand.[66]

Rithet's campaign for mayor was based on the issue of drainage, stating that the city "must be drained of its filth or it will be drained of its wealth and populace." He easily won the position, for he had always been very community minded and the citizens of Victoria had great respect for him.

In 1872, his honesty and integrity had brought him an appointment by the lieutenant-governor, Joseph Trutch, to the board of trustees in charge of lands at Ogden Point, and the following year he was made a justice of the peace. He also served one term as a member of the legislative assembly from 1894 to 1898 under then premier John Turner.

Though his involvement in business and politics often caused long absences from home, Robert Rithet still managed to maintain a happy and successful family life. His love affair with Lizzie Munro lasted a lifetime. They were a devoted couple and their marriage produced three children: Edward, who died young; John (known as Jack); and Gertrude, who married Lawrence Genge in 1904, her wedding being one of the most fashionable of its day.

Rithet and his bride had moved into Hollybank, a wedding gift from Elizabeth's father, soon after their marriage, and there the three children were born and raised. The house, at 952 Humboldt Street, was certainly one of the most elegant in Victoria, surrounded by a beautiful iron fence and the numerous holly trees from which it took its name. When Gertrude married, a house was built for her nearby on her parents's property, at 998 Humboldt, as a wedding gift. Gertrude and her mother were often seen riding their horses around their own property or across the open countryside surrounding Victoria.

Robert Rithet's additional ventures in life included numerous mining activities, as well as railway development throughout BC's interior. The building of the new dock facilities through his Wharf and Warehouse Company in Victoria ultimately led to the founding of the Canadian Pacific Navigation Company in 1883, in close association with Captain John Irving, another leading Victoria entrepreneur. Captain Irving had taken over his father's steamship company in 1872 when he was only eighteen, and by 1883 had successfully managed to merge it with that of his chief competitor, the Hudson's Bay Company. It was hardly coincidence that both Rithet and Irving had married daughters of Alexander Munro. One of their new line's fastest ships was appropriately named the *R.P. Rithet* and was the first coastal steamer equipped with hydraulic steering gear.

Rithet maintained many of his close business ties with San Francisco, and he and his family made frequent trips to that city. San Francisco's great earthquake in April 1906 caused the Rithets much grief; it was a calamitous experience to live through because of their special affection for the area. Today, a leatherbound book once kept by Robert Rithet (now in the possession of his descendants) shows that many of his business records were destroyed as a result of that earthquake and the subsequent fires in the city.

A notation in the book, signed and dated "R.P. Rithet, 6th June, 1906," reads:

> I hereby certify that the records appearing herein were taken from a Book containing the original records now transcribed herein which were so obliterated and charred by the fire which took place in San Francisco on the 18th day of April 1906, as to be useless for record purposes, and for purposes of reference the paper being brittle and breaks when used. After transcribing, the original Book was all broken and destroyed.[67]

While Robert Rithet was obviously scrupulous in his record keeping, Lizzie Rithet, like many other ladies, was equally particular in keeping scrapbooks of her favourite poetry. Cutting out and pasting such works in daintily decorated Victorian scrapbooks was a popular pastime of the day.

The Rithet family remained something of an institution in Victoria for many years, especially because they were now the new social benchmark in the city. As monied people, they were an important part of Victoria society leading into the Gay Nineties, part of a new social set that held its numerous soirées beneath gaslight chandeliers in the drawing rooms and ballrooms of all the best homes in Victoria. Their wealth had bought them the prestige that previously only a suitable background could have earned them.

Lizzie Rithet herself was regal in appearance. She was a tall, elegant woman who preferred to dress in black, and she appeared almost haughty as she swept into gatherings. She enjoyed wearing a great deal of jewellery, notably gold chains, often strung like massive ropes around her neck and hanging down to her tiny waist.

The only tragedy in the long and happy Rithet marriage had been the early death of their son Edward. Their son Jack became an exceptional athlete but was also rumoured to be a heavy drinker, and perhaps for this reason he did not inherit his father's business when Robert died in 1919 at the age of seventy-five. It was in fact Rithet's son-in-law, Lawrence Genge, and later his grandson, J.R. Genge, who took over the operations of R.P. Rithet & Co. Ltd.

Lizzie Rithet outlived her husband and all three of her children. Jack died in 1942 and Gertrude in 1945. Lizzie herself died at Hollybank in 1952 at a hundred. Since her husband's death in 1919, she had lived with a hired companion who looked after her, and had continued to hold fashionable tea parties in her drawing room until she was well into her eighties. For the last few years of her long life, she hardly ever left her bedroom suite. Only on very rare occasions would she take a walk down to the gates of her property, always supported by her two canes.

Her memory was still very clear and sharp, and she could accurately recall stories from her childhood. She remembered the day she had arrived in Victoria aboard the *Princess Royal* with her mother, sisters, and brother, to be greeted by her father, Alexander Munro, who had preceded his family to the colony. She was five years old at that time.

She remembered the acreage next to Beacon Hill Park where the Munro house had been built and where she had met and fallen in love at the age of sixteen with the handsome and gallant Robert Rithet, who came to call one day. She could also recall the building of Hollybank near her parents' home, and the many social functions within its walls through the years when she acted as hostess for her husband. In addition, she talked of the occasions when she had been a guest at some of the most elegant Nob Hill mansions in San Francisco.

A year after Lizzie Rithet's death, Hollybank was demolished to make way for commercial development, but a piece of the original iron fence was preserved and placed in the grounds of the Royal British Columbia Museum. The stables at Hollybank were one of the last remaining in Victoria. The Rithet family is commemorated throughout the city: The building at 1117 Wharf Street, which housed the offices of R.P. Rithet, was a familiar Victoria landmark; Rithet Street in James Bay and Rithetwood in Broadmead are both named for Robert Rithet; and the valuable seven hundred acres, Broadmead, where he once bred champion horses, is now a subdivision of fine homes.

The Rithets' contribution to Victoria's social life was unique. Other than the Dunsmuirs, they were the first of the entrepreneurial families to take their place in Victoria's high society. Wealth had obviously played a large part in this change of affairs. In addition, marriages among influential families such as the Munros, Rithets, and Irvings cannot be overlooked as a contributing factor.

Money and prestige had broken through the barrier of class, proving that good old-fashioned enterprise can also find a place in high circles.

# The Barnard Family

Senator G.H. Barnard.
IMAGE CVA 98108-33-3371

Sir Frank Stillman Barnard.
IMAGE CVA 98610-01-2860

[Barnard] ... made a gallant fight and the time will come when ... [his] ... action will be fully appreciated by the party which unfortunately for them as they will find out could not stand together in a trying and difficult period in its history.

—Sir Charles Hibbert Tupper, January 1902, describing the
results of a by-election involving Francis Stillman Barnard
as Conservative candidate and George Riley, the Liberal

Two nights before, the noise had been deafening. An angry mob threatening to storm the building was quite terrifying.

It was May 1915, and Frank Barnard, lieutenant-governor of British Columbia, sat in his office at Government House pondering the events that had led up to the terrible night of May 15 when news of the sinking of the *Lusitania* had reached the city. He could not, in truth, blame the people. They were justified in being disillusioned and depressed by the news coming from the war, and the *Lusitania* had merely been the catastrophe necessary to incite them to violence. One of Victoria's own, a Dunsmuir no less, had gone down with the ship.

The mob had gathered in town and marched to various buildings, leaving a path of destruction in its wake, the object of the crowd's anger being any German name or German connection.

When someone suggested they march on Government House, they had not taken much persuading. The people remembered that Frank's wife, Martha, was a Loewen, and the very sound of her maiden name was more than enough for a mob in full stride. Frank could still hear the angry shouting, the distressing abuse hurled at his beloved Martha. It had sent her to her bed, where she had remained ever since, overwhelmed by the hatred being addressed to her.

Frank had tried to explain that she was merely a scapegoat. The people hardly knew what they were saying; it was a scenario typical of mass hysteria. But his words of comfort had fallen on deaf ears. She told him she would never understand such unreasonable fury.

Now, guards were patrolling the grounds and were positioned at the gates. Things had quieted down, and Frank knew that eventually life would return to normal. Or would it? Was this, he wondered, perhaps the end of the old order? Was the attack not merely against Germany—the enemy—but also against a certain way of life that, after this terrible war was over, would no longer exist?

# CHAPTER EIGHT

# The Keystone of the Great Confederation Arch

If enterprise and spirit had penetrated the inner sanctum of Victoria's establishment, the Barnards were the final proof of what an enterprising attitude can achieve in life. Through determination and ingenuity, this remarkable family managed to reach social and political prominence by the time the city entered the twentieth century.

Their story begins with Frank Jones Barnard, a man of strong will and stamina, who was born in Quebec in 1829. He was a descendant of Francis Barnard of Deerfield, Massachusetts, who had settled in that area prior to 1642. Following the American Revolution, the Barnards moved north to live in a land still under the British Crown. Frank was barely twelve when his father died and he was forced to earn a living to help support his family; from a relatively early age, he was no stranger to hard work. He had been raised in the hardware business but could put his hand to many other things.

In 1853 he married Ellen Stillman from Ireland, and then moved from Quebec to Toronto, where business prospects looked slightly better. Not having achieved the success he sought by spring of 1859, he succumbed to gold fever and headed for British Columbia, leaving his wife and children behind and intending to establish himself before sending for them.

His journey to Victoria was unpleasant, full of the usual discomforts of the time such as the filthy quarters and bad food endured by travellers in steerage from New York to San Francisco via the Panama Canal. His first impressions of Victoria were not particularly good either. He was astounded by the crowds of gold seekers milling around the tent town, and left immediately for Yale having, by that time, only one five-dollar gold piece to his name.

His first job in Yale was to carry cordwood on his back into town, there to saw and split it. He managed to stake a small claim and make a few more dollars. Later, he obtained a job as constable at Yale, and one of his early assignments was to accompany two prisoners downriver to New Westminster. While they were resting overnight in Hope, one of the prisoners got free of his handcuffs and attacked him. After a scuffle, Frank managed to grapple with the man and recapture him, but the experience was unnerving.

In 1860, he began work as a purser on the steamer *Fort Yale*. With the money he was then making, plus some extra cash he managed to accumulate by building a trail up the Fraser River toward Boston Bar with Captain Powers of Moodyville, he was at last able to send for his wife and family. They arrived in Victoria later that year and crossed to the mainland aboard the *Fort Yale*. On the next trip, the same steamer was destroyed by a boiler explosion just below Hope. A number of people were killed, including the captain. Frank himself, as purser, was aboard at the time, and although he was thrown some distance as a result of the explosion, he was uninjured.

That same year, Barnard started an express mail service. He came up with the idea that by travelling on foot and carrying the letters on his back from Yale into the Cariboo country, some three hundred and eighty miles, he could soon monopolize the market and make a fortune. He charged two dollars for every letter he delivered and one dollar for newspapers. Sometimes he even walked the round trip.

In the winter of 1861/62, he extended his service another two hundred miles by taking on the area between New Westminster and Yale.

Late in 1862, he also established his pony express. This meant that now he took a horse along with him, not to ride, but for carrying the mail. This extended service as far as Barkerville. Back in Yale, he joined forces with Messrs. Dietz and Nelson, who operated an express business between Yale and Victoria.

The gold being taken out of Williams Creek in large quantities was also entrusted to Barnard, who had by this time established himself as the most honest and reliable of the expressmen. His only real competition in the early days had been from Billy Ballou but, in October 1862, Billy "retired from the contest with an empty purse and a broken constitution."[68]

It was said of Frank Barnard that only "through courage, vigilance, unwonted pluck, perseverance and energy, [he] . . . accomplished the perilous journeys and avoided being robbed."[69]

When the wagon road from Yale into the Cariboo was completed as far as Soda Creek, two hundred and forty miles, Barnard was finally able to officially establish Barnard's Express & Stage Line.

With the capital he had saved, plus some money from backers who were perceptive enough to see that here was a man who was definitely going places, Frank equipped himself with some splendid six-horse coaches that seated fourteen passengers and were driven by crack whips at high speeds.

One of Barnard's most famous stagecoach drivers was Steve Tingley, who would, in 1894, buy out his son and rename the company the British Columbia Express. A delightful story concerning one of Tingley's fast drives along a particularly dangerous section of the narrow, winding road through the Fraser Canyon tells of a nervous lady passenger who asked him what would happen if the coach's wheels went over the edge. Tingley's quick reply was, "Well, that, Ma'am, depends strictly upon the sort of life you've been living up to that moment."[70]

The first advertisement of Barnard's Express into Soda Creek read:

EXPRESS FREIGHT

and

PASSENGER LINE

STAGES

After the first day of May, 1864, the coaches of this line will run as follows:

UP TRIP

Leaves Yale on

MONDAYS AND FRIDAYS AT 3 AM

Passing over the

SUSPENSION BRIDGE

and

THROUGH THE CANYONS

By daylight, and reaching

SODA CREEK

In time to connect with the Stern wheel steamer

*Enterprise*

On Thursdays and Mondays at daylight, reaching

QUESNELLE CITY

on the same day.

DOWN TRIP

Leaves Soda Creek on the arrival of the *Enterprise* on Tuesdays and
Thursdays, reaching Yale on Thursdays and Saturdays in time to connect
with the steamers for New Westminster.

F. J. Barnard.

Yale, April 30, 1864.[71]

Now carrying passengers and freight in addition to mail, newspapers, and
gold, Frank was able, by 1864, to extend and improve his service even
more; two years later he bought out Dietz and Nelson and extended his
own route to Victoria. He then controlled all express services between

Victoria and Barkerville, and held the sole government contract through-out Cariboo country.

In 1868, Frank moved his family from Yale to Victoria and lived there for the rest of his life. The Barnards moved to a house on Fort Street but eventually bought Duvals Cottage on Rockland Avenue. As the house was added to, it outgrew its cottage status and became known simply as Duvals. He had always taken an interest in politics, a field in which both his sons were later to excel. In 1866, he was elected to the legislature for Yale and continued to represent that town until 1870. He also considered himself one of the prime instigators for Confederation. In 1879, he was elected to represent the Yale-Kootenay district. Frank's marriage to Ellen Stillman produced three children: Francis, born in Toronto in 1856, a daughter, Alice, in 1858, and a second son, George, born in Victoria in 1868.

The Barnards continued to prosper, barring one unfortunate business venture in which Frank was engaged in 1870. He had attempted to use steam rollers on the Cariboo wagon road. He purchased six of them from Scotland at enormous expense, only to find that they were quite unsuitable for the roads of BC; he was forced to abandon the idea and cut his losses.

In 1874, he obtained a government contract for building part of the transcontinental telegraph line, from Fort Edmonton to Cache Creek. In the long run, this too proved an expensive business because the government changed the route twice and the work was suspended for four years. Frank had laid out considerable money in advance for materials but, in 1878, the contract was cancelled and again he was forced to carry a loss.

Perhaps as a result of worry over these financial setbacks, he suffered a stroke in 1880, which left him an invalid, and he died in July 1889. Despite his failing health in those last nine years, Francis Jones Barnard retained his keen mind and active interest in many business enterprises throughout BC. He did not seek re-election at the general election in 1887 and, again because of ill health, was forced to decline a senatorship offered to him in 1888.

The eldest Barnard son, Francis, carried on his father's tradition of business initiative and political insight. His early school days were spent in Yale, and he attended the Collegiate School in Victoria from 1866 until 1870. In keeping with a popular Victoria tradition among upper-class families, he was then sent to complete his education in eastern Canada at Hellmuth College in London, Ontario.

Three years later, he returned to BC to join the family business. After his father suffered the stroke, Francis took control of the company. Still only in his mid-twenties, he managed to reverse the fortunes of Barnard's Express, which had been on the point of collapse.

In 1883, Francis formed a new company called the Victoria Transfer Company, subsequently merging it with the old one. A later plan to join a syndicate and buy out the Hastings Mills was an equally wise move, and one which renewed and re-established the family fortunes.

Meanwhile, young Francis was also enjoying an active social life in Victoria. He was one of the first members of the Union Club of Victoria, and was soon courting Martha Loewen, the daughter of Joseph Loewen, owner of the Victoria Phoenix Brewing Company. Martha and Francis were married in November 1883 in the Loewen family residence on Pandora Street, their wedding being the society event of that year. The couple lived first at Duvals, but later they acquired a home in Esquimalt overlooking the harbour, which they called Clovelly.

Like his father, Francis took an active part in the political scene. He represented the South Ward on Victoria City Council from 1886 to 1887 and stood as a Conservative candidate in November 1888 to represent Lillooet-Cariboo in the House of Commons in Ottawa. He won his seat that year and was re-elected in 1891, but in 1896 he declined to stand and retired for a while from politics. His decision was based partly on his business affairs, which kept him too busy, and partly on the fact that his brother-in-law, John Mara, was the member for Yale. It had recently merged with the Cariboo riding, and the family relationship would have caused a conflict of interest.

Meanwhile, Francis cashed in on BC's boom years and involved himself for the next while in many activiities symbolizing wealth in the province. With Mara and Captain John Irving, he founded the Columbia & Kootenay Steam Navigation Company, hauling freight on Kootenay and the Arrow lakes. He also established the Okanagan Land and Development Company, which help found the town of Vernon.

He then invested his money wisely in such companies as the Lanark Consolidated Mining & Smelting Company, and Lillooet, Fraser River and Cariboo Gold Fields Limited. Ranching was his joy, and on his seven-thousand-acre B.X. Ranch near Vernon he raised horses.

In 1894, he set up an electric power company, the Consolidated Railway & Light Company, and he soon acquired numerous other electrical companies in the province. A major setback to this venture was the collapse of the Point Ellice Bridge in May 1896, following which numerous lawsuits were filed against that company, causing it to go bankrupt.

Undaunted, Francis then proceeded to buy up all the property of his former company at a sheriff's sale. Then he and his partner, Robert Horne-Payne, a man he had met in Nelson in 1894, formed a new company in April 1897, calling it the BC Electric Company. This company was to become the forerunner of BC Hydro.

After six years away from politics, Francis suddenly felt the urge to involve himself once more and, in 1902, he stood as the Conservative candidate in a provincial by-election. He was defeated by the Liberal, George Riley, but with a difference in votes of only four hundred and twenty-one, he was thought to have done extremely well.

By now he was highly thought of in political circles and his opinions were often sought. A new order in politics was imminent. The days of "men not party" were gone, and the time had come for good party organization. Barnard was on a committee at a Conservative Party convention in 1902 that resolved to support party government for the administration of the province. Finally, the Conservative Party had a definite platform from which to work and, in early June 1903, young Richard McBride became premier of BC with this new outlook.

As for Barnard, he preferred to remain in the background, deciding never again to run for political office. Instead, he and his wife began a series of world tours, travelling extensively to numerous places throughout Europe, Australia, and Asia.

Back in Victoria, he was offered the position of lieutenant-governor of BC. He accepted the honour and took office on December 17, 1914. He and his wife especially enjoyed the social aspects of the job and entertained extensively. Two of their more important visitors were the Duke and Duchess of Connaught in 1916. In 1917, they entertained the Duke of Devonshire, and in 1918, Prince Arthur, the governor-general, thereby strengthening BC's ties with the Crown. But the visit of the Prince of Wales in September 1919 far outshone all the others. Civic functions, gala balls, and glittering banquets were all splendid. Francis Barnard was knighted in the New Year's Honours List of 1919. He retired from office at the end of the year, and the Barnards returned to Clovelly.

Only one episode had marred their time at Government House. It occurred in May 1915, when news reached the city of the sinking of the *Lusitania*. For a while, feelings ran high in Victoria against anyone with a German background, and this, of course, included Mrs. Barnard, whose father, Joseph Loewen, was of German extraction. An enraged mob first vandalized the Victoria Phoenix Brewery and two days later marched on Government House itself; threats were made against Mrs. Barnard's life. Troops were ordered to guard Government House to prevent further violence.

The mob's angry reaction had undoubtedly come about as a result of general frustration in the city, not only with the Germans' sinking of the *Lusitania*, but also the constantly depressing war news and long casualty lists reaching Victoria every day. An unfounded report had also circulated to the effect that the "society people" up at Government House had actually held a party to celebrate the birthday of Germany's emperor, and following the sinking of the *Lusitania*, Martha Barnard was said to have raised a glass in honour of the kaiser. This rumour served to incense people even more. The anger they felt can best be described as the first true outburst of hostility toward the establishment.[72]

After leaving Government House, the Barnards again travelled widely, making several more tours of Europe. They also enjoyed a happy and well-rounded retirement in Victoria, where Francis played golf and sailed. He died on April 11, 1936, at eighty.

Martha Barnard died in 1942 at seventy-six; she had had no children.

While Francis had been achieving great things in BC, his brother George (known as Harry) had been far from idle. Twelve years younger than Francis, Harry had attended the Reverend Cridge's school and later Trinity College School in Port Hope, Ontario.

At sixteen, he returned to Victoria to enter the law offices of Eberts and Tayler. Called to the bar in 1891, he later formed a partnership with E.E. Wootton and the Honourable Mr. Justice McPhillips. Eventually, he founded the law firm of Barnard, Robertson and Heisterman.

Following the strong family tradition of politics, he entered municipal politics himself in 1902 by winning the James Bay seat on city council. He was re-elected in 1903 and the following year became Victoria's twenty-fourth mayor. He was then only thirty-six. In 1905, he served a second mayoralty term.

Perhaps Harry Barnard's greatest municipal achievement was the work he did to bring the Empress Hotel to Victoria, a project he felt so strongly about that he had chosen to campaign on that issue alone; the building of the causeway and the granting of the Canadian Pacific Railway contract to build the Empress in Victoria were his pet undertakings.

He had always strongly encouraged the CPR to see Victoria as a tourist centre, and was one of the first men of vision to emphasize the potential of tourism for the city. In 1906, Harry was elected president of the Victoria Association of the Liberal-Conservative Party and two years later became president of the newly formed provincial Liberal-Conservative Association.

When Harry was elected to the House of Commons in Ottawa, defeating the Honourable William Templeman in the process, BC had only seven seats. Three of those had been filled at different times by his own family—his father, his brother, and now himself. He was re-elected in 1911 and continued to promote Victoria at all times as an ocean port. Largely at his prompting, work on the Ogden Point docks began in 1913. These enabled large liners to come into Victoria, bringing thousands of tourists with them.

In 1917, he was appointed to the Senate and said at the time that he "was glad to accept because while still interested in political affairs, I was tired, and had made up my mind not to seek re-election."[73]

Like his brother, he had a happy marriage lasting many years. He had married Ethel Rogers from Peterborough in 1895, and the young couple moved into the Barnard family home on Rockland Avenue. In fact, Harry and Ethel lived the rest of their lives on the Duvals estate, and celebrated their golden wedding anniversary there in 1945. Harry died in 1954.

Toward the end of his life, he maintained that he had found his time as a senator the most rewarding of all. "I have found life in the Senate much more peaceful than in the Commons."[74]

Despite spending thirty-seven years of his adult life as a member of one or the other of the chambers of Parliament, he never lost his optimistic outlook on political life. He made many friends on both sides and believed strongly there were good people on both sides of the House. Naively perhaps, he also believed that political corruption simply did not exist.

The third child of Francis and Ellen Barnard was a daughter named Alice. One of the grandest events to take place at Duvals was her marriage to John Andrew Mara in 1882. Mara was one of the celebrated Overlanders of 1862, who had travelled to BC by an overland route, stayed on, and eventually prospered in the province.

He was MLA for Kootenay in the first BC legislature after the province joined Confederation in 1871. He was also Speaker of the House from 1883 to 1886 and MP for Yale from 1887 to 1896.

The Barnard children had all, at one time or another, been given slices of the Duval estate, where they built their first homes. Alice and John Mara lived on the property, and there they raised their two children, a son, Lytton, and a daughter, Nellie, who later became Mrs. Alan Morkill. Both Lytton and Nellie also lived for many years on the original Barnard property.

A book in the possession of Mara descendants titled *A Historic and Present Day Guide to Old Deerfield*, written by Emma Lewis Coleman, is inscribed with the words "To G.H. Barnard from F.S.B.," dated 1927. The book was a gift that year from one Barnard brother to the other, telling stories of their ancestry in Deerfield, Massachusetts. It is symbolic of their strong belief in the importance of the past, particularly their own roots.

It also reflects the importance given to background and family at that time in Victoria's history. It was believed that these were the bonds and the foundations in life that ultimately led to stability of purpose and dedication of intent in all future endeavours.

To this belief, the early settlers in Victoria added strong marital ties between families of influence. All these ingredients, with an added flourish of initiative displayed by families such as the Rithets and the Barnards, were the essentials needed to map out a brilliant future, not only for themselves and their children, but also for BC in general.

Lieutenant Governor Sir Francis Stillman Barnard in his carriage (between 1916 and 1918).

Government House fancy-dress ball during Barnard regime (date unknown).

# INTIMATE DETAILS

In the first seventy-five years of social activity among Victoria's aristocracy, times changed considerably. From the high-jinks in Fort Victoria's Bachelors' Hall to elegant, glittering Government House balls in the early part of the twentieth century, life had progressed at a leisurely pace. The stories of the eight families discussed have shown this natural progression.

It was a fascinating social journey of discovery, set in the Victorian era when morals and standards were paramount, and customs and traditions all important. The one thing that had remained constant through it all was the strong division of the classes. It was generally accepted that every human being had his station in life. Victoria's upper-class establishment maintained this belief and strongly upheld it in all their social activities.

Their high teas, their balls, and their banquets set standards of acceptable behaviour, just as the way they dressed, how they travelled, their conversations, and their customs were all-important means of recognizing and establishing what they believed was their rightful place in society. Where they lived, whom they married, and even how they were buried were also strong indicators of their importance.

These intimate details were what set them apart and confirmed their place in the establishment.

Boats and boating, Gorge Regatta, 1890.
IMAGE A-02903 COURTESY OF ROYAL BC MUSEUM, BC ARCHIVES

# CHAPTER NINE

# Balls, Banquets, and Enlightened Entertainments

Whenever people live near each other in large numbers, especially if they are far from their original homes, sooner or later they will socialize. Over a hundred years ago in British Columbia, this was especially true among these already described upper-class families in Victoria.

That need to socialize, with luncheons, afternoon teas, balls, and dinner parties, extended to a need for entertainment. To begin with, however, certain standards of rank and position had to be firmly established. It was essential to define the boundaries so that social activity could be categorized and enjoyed within the individual classes.

F.E. Walden, in his *Social History of Victoria, 1858–1871*, wrote,

The British governing clique held firmly to its position as the upper class in Victoria. Governor Douglas and the succeeding governors, their wives and families, entertained the high supporting officials of the colony, most of whom were resident in Victoria. High-ranking officers of the Royal Navy and the Royal Engineers were included in this circle, and junior officers of the Services provided suitable escorts for the young ladies of these families. High officials of the Hudson's Bay Company completed this ruling hierarchy.[75]

Everyone belonged to a particular class, and this was clearly understood and accepted by all. One's class status dictated whether or not one was inside or outside that elusive circle described as the "ruling hierarchy."

In the days of the fort, to be inside the circle meant you were in some way connected to the Hudson's Bay Company or had come to the colony from a suitable middle- or upper-class background, and had a good education to boot.

Once one's appropriate class (in this case upper) was established, one could merely sit back and enjoy all the social activities available. And there were many. A rather flowery account in the *Colonist* of August 1890 described Victoria high society's quest for pleasure:

> Society in Victoria gave itself away to pleasure early last evening, and continued its ardent worship till an equally early hour this morning. Society bent low and devoutly before that shrine, the god of pleasure, which it so deeply adores, and thought of naught else besides. The world was forgotten for the nonce, because a call was made which demanded immediate obedience. The call was responded to most eagerly and the place resorted to was the Assembly Hall.[76]

The event the *Colonist* was referring to was a ball given in 1890 for Rear-Admiral Hotham and the officers of the Pacific Squadron, but upper-class Victoria was no stranger to such elaborate occasions.

Two early writings offer a glimpse of some of Victoria's worship of social activity in those years. The first comes from the pen of Robert Melrose, who arrived in the colony in 1853 to work as a carpenter for Kenneth McKenzie at Craigflower Farm. Strictly speaking, Melrose did not, by definition, qualify as a member of the upper-class circle, but his diary throws considerable light on how everyone, be they upper, middle, or lower class, lived and socialized at that time.

He frequently wrote about the amount of liquor consumed in Victoria, and his descriptions of Christmas and New Year's celebrations: "fiddling, eating and drinking" and "celebrated in a glorious Bacchanalian manner"[77] paint a vivid picture of the times. The only other occasions for socializing seem to have been funerals or weddings and, according to Melrose, there was certainly a plethora of both.

Martha Cheney Ella's diary (1853–56) also gives an in-depth look at life in early Victoria. Martha arrived aboard the *Tory* in May 1851 with her aunt and uncle, Thomas and Anne Blinkhorn. Still in her teens, she wrote a lively account of their farming life in Metchosin on Vancouver Island. Her diary is the only known account of life in the pre-gold rush era from a woman's point of view. Only parts of the diary have survived, written in a blue-lined scribbler; even those sections are hard to decipher.

It is especially interesting in its descriptions of Victoria's social life. Martha, like many pioneer women of that period, worked hard all day, ironing, churning butter, and being generally occupied with farming chores, but she was able to "dance until 4 o'clock in the morning at the Governor's Ball at the Fort."[78]

Much of the socializing took place in the farmhouse itself, where guests often stayed overnight and were entertained with good conversation and equally good homemade meals. Martha makes frequent mention of "a houseful of company," their farmhouse being a halfway point between the fort and Sooke.

The Royal Navy played a large role in the social life of those first colonists, like Martha Cheney and the Blinkhorns, just as it did with the Puget Sound Agricultural Company's farming families, such as the Skinners, McKenzies, and Langfords. Frequent dinner parties or balls were held aboard the visiting naval vessels, and everyone who was anyone was invited.

This is corroborated by many other accounts, one in particular by

Lieutenant Charles Wilson of the Royal Engineers in his journal. In August 1858, he wrote:

> In the evening we all went to a ball given by the officers of the *Plumper*, where we met all the young ladies of Vancouver Island, they only number about 30 and are not very great beauties, however, I enjoyed myself very much, not having had a dance for such a time. Most of the young ladies are halfbreeds and have quite as many of the propensities of the savage as of the civilized being.[79]

In a later entry, Wilson wrote:

> We are quite gay here now, nothing but Balls, private Theatricals etc., with the Flag ship and other ships there is quite a small fleet.[80]

❧

It is apparent that socializing in early Victoria took place either at the initiation of the Royal Navy or within the compounds of the fort itself. There the company men enjoyed themselves royally in Bachelors' Hall.

Captain Grant, Vancouver Island's first settler and a frequent visitor to the fort, was a good example of one settler who managed to enjoy a good social life despite the hardships and isolation of his environment. He was by nature a sociable man who sought good companions along with good whisky, and his contributions to the fort's social scene were considerable. One evening, he encouraged the younger company men to bound around Bachelors' Hall like kangaroos, supposedly imitating Queen Victoria's coach horses pulling her carriage around Windsor Park.

However, worthwhile pursuits did eventually arrive at Fort Victoria. They came in the form of cultural activities such as theatricals, a popular pastime enjoyed by many of the first colonists on Vancouver Island. The earliest recorded amateur theatrical performance given in Victoria was a production by the gentlemen of the fort in January 1857 of Sheridan's play *The Rivals*. The cast was rather grandly referred to in the program as the "dramatis personae" and included such notables as Colonial Surveyor Joseph Pemberton playing the part of Sir Lucius O'Trigger, Chief Trader J.W. McKay in the role of Sir Anthony Absolute, and Pemberton's assistant, Benjamin W. Pearse, as Fag.

The audience was also treated to an amusing prologue, which explained the play's long delay in production as due to various "duties" in which the cast had been involved and that had kept them busy. In this connection, a joke was made about each member of the cast, describing their activities at that time. This no doubt held great significance for the company men and had the crowded mess-hall at the fort rocking with laughter far into the night.

The popularity of dramatic productions continued to increase. On occasion, touring companies from San Francisco also paid visits to Victoria. Victoria liked to laugh, so comedy was always in great demand. The standard of entertainment was not particularly high, and a visitor to the city once remarked that "taste for the noblest form of the drama is not general."[81]

By 1860, the town had also been entertained to a production of *Lucretia Borgia* at the recently erected Colonial Theatre. Theatres at that time were being built at an almost alarming rate and seemed to go up virtually overnight.

In July 1862, under the patronage of Governor Douglas, a high-quality theatrical group of entertainers called the Dillon Troupe presented *Othello*, *Delicate Ground*, and *Morning Call*. It was their last performance in North America before leaving for Australia. Later productions in the city included *The Jewess* and *Judith of Geneva*.

Eventually, with fewer theatrical groups visiting Victoria, the citizens decided to form their own. They called it the Victoria Amateur Dramatic

Group, and it was composed mostly of well-educated gentlemen (no well-bred lady would have been seen dead on the stage). Membership was five dollars. Their first performance was at the Victoria Theatre in December 1862 and included two plays, *Bachelor of Arts* and *Little Toddlekins*. Governor Douglas remained as patron.

James Douglas's daughter, Martha, also enjoyed the theatre. She reports in her diary in 1867:

> This evening Papa and I went to the theatre to see a performance by the Amateur Dramatic Association for the benefit of the Fire Company. Two pieces were acted: "Time Tries All" and "Retained for Defence" with a Musical Interlude. The acting was very good, especially Miss Jenny Arnot who is very much improved in manners and appearance since I last saw her.[82]

Unfortunately, the theatres were extremely cold and often uncomfortable even for upper-class patrons, and unless one owned one's own carriage, it was difficult to travel to the theatre in time for the performance. As late as 1866, there were rarely more than six hacks available for hire.

The wealthy, however, continued to enjoy their theatrical pleasures for many years. In keeping with their simple and uncomplicated lifestyle, they also revelled in musical entertainment. Their evenings often consisted of organized musical socials in the fort or in their own homes.

The first piano to arrive on Vancouver Island came in the spring of 1855 and was the proud possession of Mrs. Mouat, wife of company man Captain W.A. Mouat. Augustus Pemberton had brought his flute from Ireland, Benjamin W. Pearse and the Reverend Cridge played violin and cello, respectively, and this completed the talented musical ensemble within the fort.

Strong interest in this type of musical soirée meant that it was not long before a philharmonic society was formed, to present more professional concerts on a regular basis. A group of musicians met in January 1859 at the home of Selim Franklin and elected officers for the newly formed society. Judge Matthew Begbie was elected president, and Franklin vice-president. The society gave regular performances, usually at the Assembly Hall on Broad Street, where they often performed to large audiences.

A cultural pursuit equally popular with the upper class was literature. Everyone loved to read, and soon the demand for books and periodicals far outweighed the supply. There appeared to be a desperate need in the early settlers not to be thought of as merely backwoods colonists. The upper class still considered themselves the intelligentsia, despite the isolation of their environment, and reading was one way to keep abreast of affairs. It was not long, therefore, before a need was seen for a library in Victoria.

Soon after the first influx of miners arrived in the spring of 1858, a Frenchman named W.F. Herre started the first library. It consisted of a reading room "in conjunction with a saloon," but according to the Victoria *Gazette*, the library was "as yet limited, but so soon as books can be obtained from San Francisco, will be greatly enlarged."[83] At least it was a beginning.

When Herre departed for France, he put his businesses, including the library, up for sale for twelve hundred dollars. Nothing more happened for a year, and then a reading room was opened by the Young Men's Christian Association. It was situated on Yates Street and later moved to the ground floor of Dr. Dickson's house on Government Street. Hours were from five to ten o'clock every evening, and the charge for membership was six shillings. The reading room was mainly stocked with religious publications, scientific papers, and periodicals from Great Britain, and it provided a place where people of all classes could go.[84]

Soon a group of interested patrons went one step further and formed the Victoria Literary Institute. Membership was five dollars, with a monthly subscription of one dollar paid by the board of directors in addition. A librarian and staff were appointed. During 1861 and 1862, a series of lectures and readings were held. They were all well attended by the town's leading and most influential people; the church, the government, the HBC, and the town's community of merchants were all represented.

Funds were raised for future readings but, although the idea had initially seemed to be popular, the Literary Institute eventually met its demise. It had, however, served a purpose in that it had brought together upper-class citizens for the benefit of good literature and stimulating company. It also set a certain standard and was a foundation from which to work.

A similar organization, which had long been popular in England, was the Mechanics' Institute. Its purpose was to "supply technical instruction to artisans . . . [and had] . . . developed into a social institution including book collections."[85] A Victoria branch of this institute opened to the public in 1864. It operated from two rooms on Langley Street and soon included a library, where cultural and scientific lectures, readings, elocution classes, and a debating club were held.[86]

The institute also sponsored such pleasurable pursuits as picnics, theatricals, and boat excursions, and organized a chess club. Picnics, in particular, had always been a favourite pastime for the settlers. An early picnic presided over by Amelia Douglas herself was described delightfully:

My first experience of a real picnic was on the occasion of one given by Mrs. Douglas to the school children at the North Dairy Farm. Dump carts, wagons and any other rough vehicles and horses were put into requisition for the conveyance of the guests on this memorable occasion. Can I ever forget the lurid happiness of that delightful day? In my boyish imagination I could not conceive anything grander, more luxurious or extravagant could be done in this world. The glorious day, the unrivalled scenery, at that time unspoilt by the hand of man, the wealth of floral beauty, the thorough enjoyment of the drive in the rough vehicles, the rich milk and cream from the dairy, the jam tarts with twisted ropes of crust over them, the cookies and unlimited bread and butter, were to my mind the acme of extravagant luxury, and lastly, the drive home in the evening concluded this never-to-be-forgotten day of happiness.[87]

Picnics continued to be fashionable in Victoria for many years. Later, those held on the lawns of Point Ellice House were among the most enjoyable, and certainly the ones at which to be seen.

Navy or military personnel also organized picnics, such as the one held on Saturday, August 1, 1885, at the Agricultural Grounds at Beacon Hill. Under the patronage of the lieutenant-governor, the picnic was billed as an "Artillery Picnic" and was held by the officers, non-commissioned officers, and men of the BC Garrison Artillery. It too was well attended.

Through the years, more elaborate amusements were added to the simple lifestyle of the original colonists. Soon there were cricket matches or the ever-popular horse races at Beacon Hill, croquet and tennis tournaments on the lawns of the most elite homes, elaborate celebrations of the Queen's Birthday in May each year, and the annual regattas along the Gorge. It was indeed a time when Victorian high society gave itself up fully to the important business of pleasurable pursuits.

In 1861, the Jockey Club was formed for the promotion of horse racing on Vancouver Island; the fee was twenty dollars. Two meetings were held annually, one in spring to coincide with the May 24 celebrations, and the other in the fall. Naval and military personnel were admitted to club membership, with the Honourable H.D. Lascelles of the Royal Navy being one of the most prominent riders for the club. Original membership indicates "a predominance of Englishmen of the official governing class, and the officers of the navy and army, with lawyers and judges admitted."[88]

The tradesman and first mayor of Victoria, Thomas Harris, was an exception to this membership rule, probably because of his obvious knowledge of and experience with horses, and his great organizational skills.

Being merely a merchant and certainly lacking in education, he would not have qualified as a member of the establishment.

Elaborate regattas organized by the Royal Navy usually took place in Esquimalt Harbour or along the arm of the Gorge. Whalers and cutters were pulled by crews over a designated course, and the races were watched by spectators from aboard launches and barges. Large crowds would also gather along the banks of the Gorge. A regatta was one of the few occasions when class distinction was often forgotten in the excitement of the moment.

One of the most spectacular regattas ever held was during Sir John A. Macdonald's visit to Victoria in 1886. On that hot August night, the waters of the Gorge were ablaze with the lights of hundreds of Chinese lanterns and torches. Over a thousand people gathered around the Point Ellice Bridge to witness the approaching flotilla making up the regatta. Next day, the *Colonist* described the procession:

> At Point Ellice hundreds of torches were blazing, making the darkness light, and the many lights rose gracefully and picturesquely into the air. Out of the darkness came the grand water pageant, moving along slowly, resembling a ship burning at sea, or a mountain flickering with the myriad lights of a host of fireflies.[89]

The Queen's birthday every May 24 was an equally important social event for Victorians, particularly those of British background. Toasts were drunk to Her Majesty's health throughout the day, while dances were held by the elite.

Most of early Victoria's upper class liked to travel abroad. Visits back to the old country and tours through Europe or the United States were the rule rather than the exception. But one excursion that took place nearer Victoria in 1879 was somewhat different and, at the time, drew considerable attention from the press.

In the *Colonist* of August 13 that year, a report announced that

> the commodious steamer *Princess Louise* will leave the Hudson's Bay
> wharf this morning on what promises to be a very pleasurable trip com-
> pletely around Vancouver Island—a great adventure.[90]

It would indeed prove to be a great adventure and, as usual, when some-
thing innovative was about to happen, many of the town's most important
citizens were involved. For this excursion, such notables as Justice and
Mrs. Crease, Captain and Mrs. Vidler, the photographers Richard and
Hannah Maynard, BC's first provincial secretary and an early mayor of
Victoria, Alexander Rocke Robertson, the fiery politician Amor de
Cosmos, another mayor Charles Redfern, and clothier William Wilson,
were all aboard.

Charles Kent and his son Herbert, both well known in musical circles
in Victoria for many years, were also among the passengers on that notable
trip. When the party returned ten days later, the younger Kent wrote a
detailed account of the adventure for the *Colonist*. His vividly descriptive
article ended:

> Thus was completed a most enjoyable excursion. All those who were on
> board speak very highly of the appointments of the splendid steamer,
> and the courteous manner in which Capt. Lewis and his officers exerted
> themselves to ensure safety and comfort.[91]

It may have been only a boat ride around Vancouver Island, but to
Victorians it was a memorable event of great importance.

It is safe to say that the elite certainly knew how to amuse themselves, but it was at their balls and banquets where they really excelled.

In the early days, all the most important balls were held aboard visiting naval vessels or in the Douglas family home on Elliot Street, which doubled as Government House. The Assembly Hall on Fort Street near Vancouver Street was also an important location for the elite to gather and dance the night away, as was Armadale, home of the MacDonald family, and Cary Castle, which later became the official Government House.

One of the most fashionable and impressive balls held in Victoria was given by Governor Kennedy in May 1866. He had purchased Cary Castle as his official residence the year before and was now eager to impress everyone with the opulence and grandeur of his station. Hundreds of invitations were sent out, not only to high society in the colony of Vancouver Island, but also to the English and American garrisons at San Juan Island. Guests were received in the drawing room by Governor and Mrs. Kennedy and their two pretty daughters. A visitor from California, referred to simply as Miss Banks, also made up the reception line.

At 9:00 PM guests were ushered into the ballroom and the first quadrille began. Between midnight and 1:00 AM, the supper room was opened up although "dancing was maintained" during the interval. Later, the governor proposed the health of the queen, and Mayor Lumley Franklin proposed the health of the governor.

"On repairing to the ballroom," wrote the *Colonist* next day, "Miss Kennedy ably presided at the piano, while the musicians partook of refreshments."[92] Dancing continued until 3:00 AM at which time the two Miss Kennedys sang the first verse of the national anthem. Mayor Franklin contributed the second verse, followed by Miss Banks with the third. The *Colonist* added that "the audience were completely electrified by the magnificent and highly cultivated voice possessed by this gifted young lady."[93]

The ball was considered a resounding success.

Another such event was held in November 1871, to celebrate the thirtieth birthday of the Prince of Wales, who later became King Edward VII. Lieutenant-Governor Joseph Trutch and his wife were the hosts at Cary Castle on that auspicious occasion, the first of many during Sir Joseph's time in office.

The following May, Government House was again the scene of a pleasant social gathering, this time a ball to mark the Queen's birthday. The Trutches sent out four hundred invitations, and the rooms were crowded to capacity with elegantly dressed ladies and gentlemen.

The Assembly Hall was the site of the spectacular ball in August 1890, given in acknowledgment of the many courtesies received by the colonists from naval representatives. This ball was

> an attempt at making the representatives of Britain's maritime power feel that, though they sojourned among colonists, their lot had fallen among British subjects, whose ambition for Britain's welfare is the same as theirs, whose hope is that they may ever continue to be one of England's most substantial bulwarks, as well as her chief colony.[94]

On such occasions, the Assembly Hall underwent a "marvelous transformation" wrote the *Colonist*. It became

> a fairyland in miniature, peopled by beings who, though manifestly material, seemed happy, every bit as ethereal beings, as they walked hither and thither with that gait and manner which, in their apparent abandon, speak of minds free from present care, past trouble, or future anxiety. Smiling faces, laughing voices, handsome uniforms, rich flowers, bright and flowing, modest flowers, shrinking and shy, vigorous flowers, braving the heat and artificial lights as naturally as though it were the place wherein they bloomed first, multi-colored flags of nations as numerous as the colors they contained.[95]

The account continued in the same sugary mixture of Victoriana, intended no doubt to titivate and stimulate the reader. Perhaps the most delightful snippet from the overly exaggerated account is the mention of the conservatory beyond the ballroom itself. It was there, stated the *Colonist*, that a "tête-à-tête could be had away from the dreamy dance, or a dance would be, as it so often is, 'talked over.'"[96] To eavesdrop on some of those conservatory conversations would have been most enlightening.

It was, however, at the many masked balls that Victoria's high society really outdid itself. At one such event held at the Crease home, Pentrelew, Augustus and Jane Pemberton's son Chartres dressed as Christopher Columbus, his cousin Fred Pemberton as an outlaw, and a third cousin visiting from England (with the delightful name of Perfect) was outfitted as an Italian peasant.

The masquerade ball in 1899 in aid of the Royal Jubilee Hospital was probably the event of the century for high society in Victoria. It certainly had everyone talking for weeks in advance, and no doubt while costumes were being decided upon and made by the seamstresses, books such as *Weldon's Practical Fancy Dress for Ladies and Gentlemen* were referred to.

Again the ball was to take place at Assembly Hall, and headlines in the *Colonist* the following day read, "Masks and Merriment sweet pleasure was Queen—brilliance unsurpassed—entertainment enchanting."

All the most important people in Victoria were present, although one would have been hard pressed to recognize any of them. The Pemberton family was well represented and magnificently attired. Mr. and Mrs. Fred Pemberton were dressed as a Viking and The Lady of Seville. Other family members were garbed as Madame de Pompadour, Chaseur d'Amérique, and in a costume from the First Empire (in white and silver).

Miss Maude Dunsmuir was dressed in pale blue gauze as Desdemona and Miss Birdie Dunsmuir as Cigarette from Ouida's *Romance*. Noel Harvey, a Dunsmuir granddaughter, came as a pink carnation.

Mrs. Harry Dallas Helmcken arrived as a court lady of the early empire, and Mrs. Dennis Harris (James Douglas's youngest daughter) was dressed in "magnificent brocade, becoming her statuesque beauty well." Mr. and Mrs. Harry Barnard were present, she attired in a peasant costume from the province of Vladivostock. Mrs. Herbert Kent was dressed as a yacht girl, Reginald Hayward as a Heidelberg student and his sister Florence as Economy. Even the famous architect, Samuel Maclure, and his wife were present, she dressed "in a splendid characterization of the Old Lady, wrinkles, eyeglasses and ear trumpet not forgotten."[97] The upper-class socialites were nothing if not imaginative.

They also liked to eat. Their dinner parties and banquets were perfect examples of the enormous amount of food they consumed. For instance, to mark the occasion of the Victoria Board of Trade obtaining its own building on Bastion Square in May 1893, an elaborate ten-course banquet was held and continued far into the early hours of the next morning. Among the illustrious guests enjoying the plentiful fare were Premier Theodore Davie, Robert Beaven (leader of the Opposition), Lieutenant-Governor Edgar Dewdney, financier A.C. Flumerfelt, Chief Justice Sir Matthew Begbie, industrialist Jacob Hunter Todd, and business tycoons David Ker and Robert Rithet. When the company finally rose to sing "God Save the Queen" at 4:00 AM, many of them could barely stand.

Dinner parties were held on a regular basis in the homes of the elite. The O'Reilly family, in particular, entertained on a large scale and retained all their dinner menus. They ate a great deal of lamb, roast fowl, and curried lobster, and their favourite desserts were "puddings"—marmalade, ginger-bread, or jam roll being top priorities.

A list of the retail grocery prices in January 1892 shows that three assorted jams could be purchased for one dollar; lemons from Sicily cost fifty cents each whereas from California they could be had for thirty-five cents. Reindeer milk (in tins) cost twenty-five cents and a fresh tin of oysters went for seventy-five cents. Fresh eggs were fifty cents a dozen.[98]

One of the most enlightening glimpses into how and what Victoria's upper-class citizens ate comes from the Barnard Family Collection. Lady Barnard kept a dinner party record book at the turn of the century, describing in detail the parties held both at Clovelly and at Government House during her husband's sojourn there as lieutenant-governor.

Her record book is delightfully inscribed at the beginning with a quotation from Byron:

> That all-softening, over powering knell, The tocsin of the soul—the dinner bell.[99]

Indeed, if the record book is to be believed, the dinner bell must have sounded on a multitude of occasions. Each dinner party is described in detail with the date, the occasion, the guests present, the seating arrangements, and the menu itself. A particular added delight is a notation concerning "particulars of table decoration." If, for instance, it was springtime, primroses and daffodils were in profusion on the table. Yellow roses were featured in summer, carnations and chrysanthemums in fall. At Christmas, holly was always in abundance as a centrepiece.

At Clovelly, the guests frequently enjoyed caviar followed by a consommé or cream soup, sautéed chicken, roast lamb, and asparagus. Dessert would often be rhubarb tart or chocolate pudding followed by cheese straws and ice cream. Other favourites were boiled salmon and roast duckling, and oysters on the half shell were frequently included.

At Government House, Lady Barnard continued to enjoy her dinner parties and always made a special point of decorating her table to suit the occasion or the visiting dignitaries. In April 1915, when the Japanese high commissioner visited Victoria, her table was set with Japanese cherry blossoms.

Between 1916 and 1919, the Barnards also entertained many royal personages, including the Duke and Duchess of Connaught, Princess Patricia, the Duke of Devonshire, HRH Prince Arthur, and HRH the Prince of Wales. For all the royal visits to Government House, she meticulously kept account of the dinner parties, noting on her table plan where everyone was to be seated. She even mentioned those guests unable to attend. That column was rarely filled, however, because an invitation to a Barnard dinner party was something one did not decline.

Many of the upper-class ladies of early Victoria were often thought to be idle, contained as they were in their luxurious lifestyles. A rather snobbish attitude to their servants or those of an inferior station, and the fact that they seemed to be concerned only with trivial matters such as their at-homes or their afternoon teas, tended to give the impression of laziness,

In many ways, however, it was a frustrating time for women, and even those who wished to occupy their days with other things were limited to activities such as gardening, painting, music, or helping charitable organizations. Those were thought to be the only occupations in which ladies should be involved.

The Alexandra Club, which officially came into existence on August 17, 1900, served many purposes, not the least of which was to occupy those upper-class women in more worthwhile pursuits. The club interested itself in music, literature, and the arts by introducing and sponsoring young artists and bringing them to the attention of the public.

A proclamation issued that August stated:

We the undersigned hereby agree to form ourselves into a club for the use of the ladies, to be called The Ladies' Club under the direction of a committee to be elected by a majority of the subscribers hereto. That we agree to pay an entrance fee of five dollars with a month's subscription of one dollar payable quarterly in advance. It is further understood that as soon as fifty intending members have subscribed to this paper, a meeting will be called of the same with the object of electing a committee . . . for carrying out our desired purposes.[100]

With those words, the first women's club in Victoria came into being. There were already fifty-six signed-up members, all anxious to be a part of the organization. Numbered among them were three Dunsmuir women, Mrs. Harry Barnard, Mrs. Powell, Mrs. Pemberton, Mrs. Dennis Harris, Mrs. Dewdney, and Mrs. Prior. The majority of Victoria's most fashionable families were represented at the club by their women.

Although first and foremost a social club, it also served in other capacities, doing much useful work. The Ladies' Club later changed its name to the Alexandra Club to honour Queen Alexandra, wife of the then-reigning monarch, Edward VII.

The first clubrooms were in a building at the corner of Fort and Government streets, directly above Charles Redfern's jewellery and silver store. A steep, winding staircase led up to the quiet, dignified atmosphere of the club, where ladies could sit and read, take afternoon tea, watch the world go by from the windows, or discuss, in hushed tones, the charitable projects in which they were involved. At last, being part of an organization such as the Alexandra Club, they felt needed and somewhat important. In particular, they enjoyed the feeling of belonging to a club where they could go and discuss matters of significance.

It was soon decided to build a more prestigious clubhouse, an idea initiated by Mrs. Hazell, wife of Dr. Hazell of the Royal Jubilee Hospital. Mrs. James Dunsmuir advanced the money, and construction of the Alexandra Clubhouse began immediately.

The new clubhouse stood at 716 Courtney Street and was later known as the Windermere Building. It was furnished with the very finest of everything; meals were served on elegant china, and the silverware was polished and sparkling.

The first fundraising function of the club was, naturally enough, a ball. The clubhouse was decorated for the event with a profusion of flowers, and the ladies, wearing their most beautiful gowns, arrived with their escorts. The event was the first of many.

Balls, literary events, receptions, musical evenings, and weddings were just a few of the occasions in which the Alexandra Club involved itself. A particularly memorable event was a reception given by way of farewell for Lady Goodrich, wife of the admiral at Esquimalt. The Royal Navy was making its departure from the west coast, and Canada was about to take care of its own defences. The Alexandra Club wanted to mark the occasion with a happy reminder of Victoria's association with navy personnel.

For many years, club members continued to enjoy the elegance of the environment they had created. It was a graceful era, hard to imagine in today's world. Scattered on occasional tables, amidst the potted palms in that ethereal atmosphere, were copies of many old-country magazines such as *Ladies' Field* or the *Illustrated London News*. Described in the newspapers of the day as a club housed in one of the finest buildings in Victoria, the Alexandra Club appealed to all the most influential women.

As in all things, however, times change, and even prosperity and elegance eventually disappeared in the general cycle of life. As war clouds began to appear in 1914, it became obvious that this was no longer a time for frivolous pursuit and reckless spending, even though many of the club's functions had been fundraisers. Now the ladies of Victoria turned their attentions to more serious endeavours. Some members joined the Red Cross or the Victorian Order of Nurses, and many organized fundraising events to further the patriotic cause.

Garden party at Rogers Farm, 1915—raising funds for the Red Cross.
IMAGE 1978-003-002 SAANICH ARCHIVES

The club's expenses continued, but money was no longer available. Soon it was necessary to sell the clubhouse on Courtney and move to a smaller location at the top of the Campbell Building. Here there was less space, but the ladies continued to carry on their club activities, albeit on a smaller scale. On one occasion they invited Mrs. Pankhurst to be a guest speaker. Later the club was forced to move yet again, this time to the Bank of Toronto Building. But the end was near. By this time, the Union Club of Victoria, that inner sanctum of masculine pomposity, was finally beginning to open its doors to its members' wives, many of whom were also Alexandra Club members. So, despite the demise of the Alexandra Club one year after its last move, the ladies still had somewhere to gather and discuss the events of the day. The Alexandra Club had served its purpose by successfully filling a very necessary spot in a world of grace that no longer existed. As late as the 1950s, some of the elegant Alexandra Club china, engraved with the club's initials, was still being used at functions in Victoria.

Another early Victoria club, of a different genre, was the Arion Club. Launched at the initiation of thirteen gentlemen in February 1893, its purpose was "the study of music for male voices and also for the culture and development of a refined musical taste in its members."[101] The members performed their first formal concert on May 11 of that year in the Institute Hall on View Street. The concert was attended by ladies and gentlemen of Victoria, who all came formally dressed to witness the many talents of "the young gentlemen." By the time of that May concert, membership had reached twenty-four and included such important names as George Jay (known for his work on the Victoria School Board and after whom George Jay School is named), Herbert Kent (who was destined to sing with the Arions for sixty years and become the club's historian), James S. Floyd (Oak Bay's one-time municipal clerk and a director of the Christ Church Cathedral Choir), and Ernest Wolff, local violinist, whose niece, Alma Clarke, became notorious as Francis Rattenbury's second wife and the lover of a nineteen-year-old chauffeur who murdered Rattenbury in a fit of passion.

They were a colourful and very talented group of men, and their frequent concerts through the years were always well received by members, associates, and later the general public. Associate membership extended to many of Victoria's social set, including Sir Matthew Begbie, Canon Beanlands, Henry Crease, and Mrs. Dennis Harris. By the 1936/37 season, associate membership also included Lady Barnard, Mrs. James Dunsmuir, Sir Richard and Lady McBride, and the Honourable T.D. Pattullo. Even ladies were permitted to sing with the male choir on occasion, but in the concert programs they were usually billed as "female guest artists" or "young lady amateurs."

On May 14, 1993, yet another Arion concert marked the completion of a hundred years of singing by a unique musical organization that had survived a depression, two world wars, and at least sixteen different conductors[102]—a truly remarkable achievement and a proud relic of that world of social elegance in long-ago Victoria.

If one cares to ponder social activities from that other era, there is one more delightfully coy and tantalizing source, typically Victorian in content. It was known as the *Victoria Home Journal*, a gossip newspaper published in Victoria during the 1890s, intended above all else to tease and tantalize. By its own admission, it was totally "devoted to social, political, literary, musical, and dramatic gossip."[103]

There was a column, "Society," that told of the goings-on of the upper-class set. Its charm lay in the fact that it merely hinted, in a mysteriously intriguing manner, at what was taking place around the city. It never stated complete facts, and many of its reports began with the words "rumour has it." Names were never mentioned, and the leading players in each story were described in cleverly disguised ways.

"A well-known Victorian, prominent in yachting circles will shortly wed the leading soprano singer of St. Andrew's Cathedral choir," read one report. Others stated that "the marriage of a well-known druggist to a fair young lady of this city is announced to take place in June"; "There will be a fashionable wedding at Christ Church Cathedral soon. Both of the high contracting parties are popular in society circles"; "The wedding of a prominent young barrister to an equally prominent society belle will be the matrimonial event of next week." Less flattering reports were also written on occasion. In its day, the *Victoria Home Journal* was probably the equivalent of the most shocking tabloid stories a hundred years later. The *Journal* also had a column titled "Of Interest to Women," consisting of enlightening words of encouragement for women who might need advice on otherwise unmentionable subjects such as marital or health problems.

Architect's drawing of proposed new clubhouse for Ladies' Club on Courtenay Street.
VCA 98410-10-643

Cast of a Grecian play-theatrical at the Pemberton estate, Gonzales (date unknown).
VCA 98202-25-4576

Typically large upper-class wedding party—Jessie Dunsmuir/Richard Musgrave wedding showing six bridesmaids, two flower girls, and twenty matrons of honour in attendance. September 1891.

Major social event of 1878—marriage of Martha Douglas (daughter of Sir James Douglas) to Dennis Harris.

Wedding of Canon Arthur John Beanlands to Sophie Pemberton.
IMAGE 1-46770 COURTESY OF ROYAL BC MUSEUM, BC ARCHIVES

The *Journal* could be purchased for a yearly subscription of one dollar and found its way into many a home in Victoria in the Gay Nineties. Perhaps its most important contribution was the fact that it endeavoured to keep the ladies and gentlemen of Victoria up to date on fashion. The "Clothes" column was an invaluable source of information for them and was read religiously by those who wanted to keep abreast of the times.

The way the upper class dressed had, after all, always been of paramount importance, ever since the days of the fort. The fact that these settlers had chosen to live many thousands of miles away from world fashion centres like Paris or London did not deter them from making sure they always dressed in the most current fashions and appeared presentable, as befitted their station in life, on every occasion.

Tea in the garden at Helmcken House, 638 Elliott Street (c. 1900).
IMAGE 1981-019-029 SAANICH ARCHIVES

# CHAPTER TEN

# Costumes, Conveyances, and Conversations

Appearance! To most of the upper social set in early Victoria, it was of the utmost importance. How one appeared in public or how one presented oneself to the outside world was the driving force behind most of their social activity.

With so many formal occasions to attend from the days of the fort on, there was never a time when it was not essential to be well turned out. Ladies did not want to be thought of as mere backwoods women, and gentlemen most certainly wanted their womenfolk to be not only presentable but perhaps a little above average. Judging by the flowery descriptions of ladies' gowns in the newspapers of the day, especially for weddings, the situation from the very beginning took on almost a competitive element.

Isaac Singer had patented the first sewing machine around 1851, and these new-fangled machines were finding their way to far-flung places like Victoria, which helped the fashion situation enormously. In addition, by 1863 Ebenezer Butterick had perfected the paper pattern. The first one, made of stiff paper, was put on the market that year and was a great success. By the following year, Butterick and his wife were making patterns for children's clothes from tissue paper. Salesmen were reporting a great demand for women's clothes, and soon the Buttericks were mass-producing their patterns to meet this demand. By 1869 they had founded a fashion magazine, later called *The Delineator*.

The sewing machine and the paper pattern were two very progressive steps in the dressmaking industry and meant that, by the 1870s, with the help of their seamstresses, the ladies of Victoria were able to increase their wardrobes speedily. It was now possible to have clothes made in the city, instead of having to travel abroad to buy in quantity, or send to London and Paris for gowns once the latest collections were released.

For the first twenty years of Victoria's existence, most ladies suffered the indignities of the crinoline for both day and evening wear. The crinoline skirt was anything but practical. It was cumbersome and awkward, with four narrow steel hoops running through the petticoats. Some ladies discarded the hoops but insisted on wearing stiff muslin petticoats to create the same effect. Either way, they often carried around with them at least sixteen yards of heavy, bulky material that was virtually impossible to organize into a comfortable sitting position.

The Douglas girls did not cope well with their crinolines, as can be seen from a journal entry made by one of the British officers at the time:

> They [the governor's daughters] had just had some hoops sent out to them and it was most amusing to see their attempts to appear at ease in their new costume.[104]

It was hardly surprising that by the early 1870s, the crinoline had all but disappeared in favour of a straighter style of skirt, but the change caused many ladies to feel vastly underdressed. They now had a mere ten yards of material in their gowns.

However, that early fullness in the skirt had simply changed position. The new fashion was called the bustle, placed at the rear of the skirt in the area where one would normally have sat. The bustle was worn high or low depending on the social standing of the lady's husband. It was created with the aid of wires or steel and was often so heavy that it required the support of a harness from the shoulders. It was not until well into the 1880s that fashion designers began to see the wisdom of a more simple line in women's apparel.

When common sense finally prevailed, many women in Victoria must have breathed a sigh of relief. After years of struggling with constrictive undergarments, hooped skirts requiring yards of expensive material that could be ruined by one misguided step on a mud-soaked city street, and uncomfortable areas in the rear of their gowns virtually restricting any ability to bend, women could at last enjoy a far more comfortable line. Ankle-length skirts and shirt blouses came about mainly as a result of women's eventual participation in sporting events. And a move toward a looser Grecian line for evening wear made social life far more pleasant for the Victorian lady of the 1880s.

Couturiers were soon establishing themselves around the world. Names such as Paquin, Doucet and Callot Soeurs became famous. One of the best-known men's tailors in London, the House of Creed, opened a shop in Paris in 1854 and then progressed from men's clothes to riding outfits for the Empress Eugénie and ultimately to beautifully tailored suits for women.

The Centennial Exposition in Philadelphia in 1876 offered Americans their first opportunity to see the French fashions. Custom dressmakers with a wealthy clientele regularly travelled from North America to Europe in order to bring back the very latest in fashion and then copy it for their clients, using the best of French fabrics. Sometimes the seamstresses who visited Victoria's upper-class ladies in the spring and fall each year used their creativity by taking an original skirt from one design, a sleeve from another, and a neckline from a third, and incorporating them all into a unique gown that they quite accurately labelled "one of a kind."

The introduction and brief popularity of bloomers was another innovation brought about by women's interest in sporting activities. Many of Victoria's ladies who took up bicycling at the turn of the century, for instance, enjoyed wearing them.

When an 1893 edition of *Vogue* magazine showed a woman dressed in a shooting outfit with her skirt reaching only to her calves, it might have been considered a move in a new direction. The lady was, however, wearing high boots to cover what would otherwise have been an area of exposed leg. Nevertheless, it was a statement by women who longed for a freer, more practical fashion.

Meanwhile, Charles Dana Gibson began making sketches of what he dubbed his Gibson Girl style, a definite American look, showing athletic young women dressed in shirtwaist outfits, boyish collars, puffed sleeves, and flaring, stiffened skirts. Sometimes he included a straw sailor hat. The Gibson Girl look was the beginning of ready-to-wear clothing in the American textile industry.

Yet another important event occurred in 1884. A French scientist, Count Hilaire de Chardonnet, developed rayon, the first of the man-made fibres. An artificial silk, rayon (its trade name) was made from the cellulose of pine, hemlock, and spruce trees.

The first few years of the twentieth century leading up to the First World War were carefree times in most parts of the world. There were no wars or depressions going on, so the rich were able to enjoy a constant round of pleasurable pursuits without fear of reprisal, and fashion trends tended to reflect this halcyon mood.

In Victoria, ladies continued the tradition of calling on their friends, arriving in their splendid carriages and, later, in their equally flamboyant motor cars. The clothes they chose for such pursuits were made of adaptable broadcloth and lace. For driving in those first automobiles, many ladies chose a linen duster outfit, which also served as protection from the dusty roads, and a bonnet tied with ribbon under the chin, which preserved many an elegant coiffure. For receiving at home, taffeta was a popular fabric choice. Fashion was greatly influenced, then as now, by famous personalities seen on stage or by other important members of high society, and trends still largely revolved around what was happening in Paris.

The new century brought with it small waists, puffed sleeves, and merry widow hats trimmed with ostrich feathers to create and enhance a lady's appearance in a supposedly romanticized way. By 1908, with skirts now at ankle length, there was also a brief revival of the once-popular Empire line.

Between 1910 and 1914, many women followed the latest fashion trend and hobbled about in long, narrow skirts. Eventually, by the beginning of the First World War, skirts had once again become fuller and even shorter.

Three fashion houses had revolutionized the industry during those years. The first was Jeanne Lanvin, a couturière who opened her own establishment in 1890 and created, with her own hands and scissors, all her designs. Poiret began in 1910 and soon became known for his bold and exciting colours on Oriental backgrounds, his numerous trimmings, and his use of lamé (a fabric woven with metal thread) for evening wear. He also campaigned against the use of the corset and encouraged women to abandon all their most restrictive and uncomfortable undergarments. His new, looser line led to what eventually became known as the "debutante slouch." A third great influence in the fashion industry was Madeleine Vionnet, who opened her house in 1912 and was the first to introduce the bias cut. This emphasized the line and cut of the garment, rather than its trimming, a concept that has survived.

And back in Victoria, how were the ladies in those important aristocratic circles keeping up with the latest fashions? When not poring over *The Delineator, Vogue*, or the ever-popular *Weldon's Practical Fancy Dress for Ladies and Gentlemen*, they were, during the 1890s, avidly reading the

*Victoria Home Journal.* By so doing they could easily find out the very latest thing happening in the fashion world.

There they discovered, for instance, that silk Roman sashes were all the rage. The sashes came in all tints of the rainbow, often with a deep silk fringe, and made a graceful drapery for an overly plain evening gown. Trimmings, especially feathers, were highly thought of. Clever rosebud creations were made with pink ostrich feathers and became exquisite decoration for any evening gown in pink or pale grey. The Grecian robe-style gown was worn often with its silken petticoats made of Amour, a new fabric that was thicker but softer than taffeta.

The latest Paris Opera coats arrived in Victoria during those years. They were made of cloth, with tan being the most popular colour choice. If a lady preferred to wear a cape, it was often an elaborate garment, graduated in length and trimmed with mink. A high Medici collar also edged with mink set off the cape, which was invariably lined with silk in a pastel colour. Around that same time period, wrappers were also very popular. These were dainty, airy, creations worn over a night robe, often made in accordion-pleated India silk.

Another theme in day or evening wear was to enhance a gown with tiny bows on sleeves or around hemlines. Pink crepe de Chine was favoured for evening gowns, while cloth day dresses still boasted the ever-popular leg o' mutton sleeves.

Mourning wear was mostly made of black crepe, which had a dull crinkled effect. For half-mourning, black satin or large black and white plaids were acceptable. And a true lady was rarely seen in public without a hat, no matter what the occasion.

Fashion for men, on the other hand, changed very little through the years save for a few minor exceptions. Gentlemen in the 1860s, 1870s, and 1880s wore elegant top hats and black overcoats with velvet collars for most occasions. Queen Victoria's consort, Prince Albert, gave his name to the famous double-breasted frock coat that was popular for many years. Waistcoats and stiff collars were always worn, even for the most casual events.

Children were invariably dressed as elaborately as their parents, with little thought for the possibility of playtime or getting dirty. Little girls were outfitted in party dresses of silk and satin with numerous bows, ribbons, ruffles, and pleats. Small boys wore their Eton-collared Norfolk jackets, and knickers made of tweed.

Thus, even in Victoria, high-society fashion from the 1850s onwards was elaborate, formally stiff, and largely dictated by Paris trends. Perhaps the most overpowering influence through those years was an Englishman, Charles Frederick Worth, the man who can be credited with having begun the whole adventure into the world of haute couture. Worth originally came from London in 1846 to join a Parisian silk house and later established his own enterprise in that city. He was the first designer to show his creations on live models and the first who dared to dictate to his customers what they should or should not be wearing.

He was appointed court dressmaker to the Empress Eugénie in 1860 and was said to have been the main instigator of the famous hoopskirt crinoline. It is believed that he created it to camouflage the fact that the empress was expecting an heir. His wide-skirted, off-the-shoulder lace creations, known as Winterhalter gowns, were frequently worn as wedding dresses, and his lace flounces were particularly popular following the Empress Eugénie's appearance in a ball gown that was said to contain at least a hundred and thirteen of them.

Every bride in Victoria who could afford it had her trousseau made by the House of Worth, and others also ordered their day and evening gowns; to be attired in a Worth creation was a status symbol. There were many daughters in the first families of Victoria at that time, so naturally there were also many weddings. This, of course, meant that a large number of very elaborate dresses for brides and bridesmaids were constantly being made, and descriptions of some of these dresses found their way into the newspapers. Today, family collections in the British Columbia Archives also hold detailed descriptions of some of the wedding outfits of the times.

When Jane Brew married Augustus Pemberton in 1861, for instance, her two flower girls were Martha Douglas and Amy Helmcken, and later Martha recalled and clearly described their outfits. They were made of white silk with matching white silk stockings, white kid slippers and white kid gloves. Their white bonnets had broad satin ribbons tied under the chin and pretty little wreaths of clematis around the face.

Some years later, in March 1878, Martha married Dennis Harris. Her father had already died, so she was escorted to the Reformed Episcopal Church by her brother, James. Her own gown was of rich white satin, trimmed with white tulle and orange blossoms. Her white tulle veil fell in graceful folds around her face and was held in place by a wreath of orange blossom. Martha had ten bridesmaids, each dressed in white tarlatan (a stiff, woven gauze) with ivy trimmings. They all wore wreaths of orange blossom. Three groomsmen completed the wedding party.

One of the largest weddings was that of Jessie Dunsmuir to Sir Richard Musgrave. Jessie's gown was made of white and silver brocade with a full court train decorated in silver in the pattern of the Prince of Wales crest. Her veil and trimmings were of Honiton lace. Six bridesmaids wore dresses of white Charlotte Corday fabric, with long sashes and flowers to match. There were also two train bearers, two flower girls, and another twenty young ladies acting as maids of honour, an impressively large group rarely matched by society weddings at that time.

Thomas Skinner's granddaughter, Emily Sophie (daughter of Constance and Alexander Davie), wore a gown of cream brocade trimmed with tulle and pearl embroidery for her wedding to barrister A.E. McPhillips at

St. Andrew's Cathedral in 1896. Her bridesmaids wore dresses of white China silk trimmed with silver braid.

Two O'Reilly weddings, Caroline Trutch to Peter O'Reilly, and Mary Beresford Windham to Arthur John O'Reilly, show an equal display of wedding splendour. Caroline's dress was of white brocaded silk embellished with orange blossoms. Mary's was white charmeuse (a crepe satin material) with orange blossom accessories. A veil of old Brussels lace that had been in the Windham family for many generations completed her outfit. Her going-away gown was made of crimson rattine (a blend of silk and wool), trimmed with black velvet. To top it all off she wore a brown silk hat with decorative ostrich feather and a handsome grey squirrel coat.

When Alice Barnard married John Andrew Mara in the drawing room of Duvals in 1882, her gown was of white corded silk with a train embroidered and trimmed in satin and lace. Alice, had only one bridesmaid, whose dress, surprisingly, was a blue silk and net.

Gertrude Rithet's wedding to Lawrence Genge in 1904 was another memorable event in the city and provided an unprecedented display of gowns of splendour. Gertrude's was of white crepe de Chine trimmed with duchess lace, and she carried a shower bouquet of roses, while her bridesmaids' gowns ventured again into the world of colour. As a general rule, bridesmaids then were attired in traditional whites and creams, which acted as a complement to the white gown of the bride; a dress of colour was thought to be too bold a contrast to an ensemble where the primary purpose was to show off and enhance the bride. Gertrude's bridesmaids, however, were attired in dresses of Nile green, complete with white chiffon fichus (triangular-shaped shawls) and picturesque poke bonnets.

Not only wedding dresses attracted attention in that long-ago era. When one of Victoria's native daughters, an O'Reilly no less, was about to be presented at court, her gown was of paramount interest. Kathleen O'Reilly's presentation dress still exists today but in a somewhat fragile condition and much altered from its original design. It was the very height of fashion, and Kathleen herself in correspondence with her parents described it as her "sparkley white dress."

For that momentous trip to England and Ireland in 1896 and presentation at the Irish court in February 1897, Kathleen took with her an extensive wardrobe. She described her dress in more detail as "my white ball dress covered with lilies of the valley and a train in white, lined with a delicate shade of apple green, trimmed with tulle, lilies, and white and green bows of ribbon." She added that it was "so very young looking that a girl of seventeen could have worn it."[105] She herself was already in her late twenties.

A gradual decline in the more flamboyant aspects of fashion down through the years, as well as a lack of interest in the clothing worn by the society families, is reflected in an incident in 1952. An auction was held that summer at Hollybank following the death of Elizabeth Rithet earlier in the year. Many Rithet treasures were put on the block, including Lizzie Rithet's once-valuable full-length coat of rich Alaska seal with collar and cuffs of mink. In her heyday, Lizzie was often seen wearing it at the most fashionable of society occasions. At the auction, it sold for a mere thirty-five dollars.

εℭↄ

To be well dressed was one thing but, important though that was, there was yet another aspect of life among the elite that was perhaps of equal importance: the business of travel.

As today's transportation is undertaken with such speed and comparative comfort, it is hard to imagine the inconveniences and hardships that early settlers in Victoria must have experienced. The first to arrive on Vancouver Island were limited to three alternatives—foot, horse, or boat—and each was embarked upon with a great deal of trepidation and discomfort.

Emily Carr describes the situation amusingly in *The Book of Small*. She claims that "there was no way to get about young Victoria except on legs—either your own or a horse's."

Horses did not apparently roam and had to be kept handy at all times for hitching. In Carr's chapter on "ways of getting around," she continues:

> All the vehicles used were very English. Families with young children preferred a chaise, in which two people faced the horse and two the driver. These chaises were low and so heavy that the horse dragged, despondent and slow.
>
> Men preferred to drive in high, two-wheeled dogcarts in which passengers sat back to back and bumped each other's shoulder blades. The seat of the driver was two cushions higher than that of the other passengers. Men felt frightfully high and fine, perched up there cracking the whip over the horse's back and looking over the tops of their wives' hats. There were American buggies, too, with or without hoods, which could be folded back like the top of a baby's pram.[106]

It would seem, according to Carr, that nobody in Victoria was in a hurry, and people drove mainly for the simple pleasure of enjoying fresh air and pleasant scenery.

As the city grew, and especially as the female population increased, owning a more elaborate carriage or hiring one became a necessity among the elite. There were at one time at least ten livery stables in Victoria. The Eureka Stable was a brick building on Pandora Avenue, owned by John Dalby. In addition, Dalby ran a daily stage out to Goldstream.

Bowman's Stable at Broad and View streets operated with thirty-five horses and carried mail to Esquimalt, as well as running a hack service. Yet another stable was owned by Francis Jones Barnard, who later formed the Victoria Transfer Company for the purpose of constructing and operating "street railways in the City of Victoria and Esquimalt and Victoria Districts adjacent thereto, and carrying on a general transfer, delivery, hack and livery business in the Province of British Columbia."[107]

By the 1880s and 1890s, with hack driving a large part of downtown business, health problems were also making themselves apparent. "The cab-stand on Government Street is highly objectionable,"[108] announced medical health officials in 1894. The reason was a sanitary one: with horses occupying the site for most of the day, a great deal of manure would accumulate and, when it dried, various unpleasant pieces of refuse could be seen blowing in all directions whenever there was a strong wind.

Three years after the establishment of the Victoria Transfer Company in January 1883, the company had become prosperous. Beginning with a mere fifteen horses, six buggies, and four carriages, by 1886 it consisted of "large and commodious stables covering 66 x 190 feet, at a cost of about $8,000." The stables still had a "scarcity of room for their large and continually increasing stock of horses, carriages and wagons."[109] Stock by then included over sixty horses, twelve hacks, thirty buggies and phaetons, eight omnibuses, and a number of wagons. The new omnibuses, although at first running at a loss, were gradually becoming very popular with the public at large.

By far one of the most enterprising of the carriage and hack businessmen was George Winter. In colonial days, he had been coachman to two royal governors, Kennedy and Seymour, and had later driven for Lieutenant-Governor Trutch. After Trutch left office in 1876, Winter decided to go into business for himself, but still contracted to drive for two later lieutenant-governors, Richards and Cornwall. George Winter was born in 1839 in England and joined the British navy in his teens. He arrived in Esquimalt Harbour aboard HMS *Bacchant* in 1861 and, like many others before him, decided to jump ship and join the Cariboo gold rush. He soon tired of the miner's life, however, so he returned to Victoria, married Margaret Orrick, and decided to settle. When he became coachman at Cary Castle, he and his family lived in a cottage on the grounds. Later, the Winters moved to Ross Bay and there George was able to keep horses and have space for his own carriages, once he was in business on his own. He employed a large staff to keep his carriages in immaculate condition, their brass and plate-glass lamps highly polished at all times.

Soon it became something of a status symbol in Victoria to hire a Winter carriage. They were, after all, the very last word in elegance and the company claimed it could provide "conveyances for every occasion." For dances, the theatre, weddings, or christenings, a Winter carriage was essential. To be seen driving in one, with a coachman dressed in blue, brass-buttoned livery, was to have arrived. Another attraction of Winter Carriages was the fact that they catered to their clients for specific occasions. For weddings, the carriage conveying the bride would be lined with white satin ruffles. In winter, when the snow was knee-deep, a Winter sleigh could be hired complete with bells, blankets, and heavy fur robes. Hot bricks tucked under the feet were an added touch as sleighs set off into the country. If stops were made along the way at a roadhouse, the gentlemen in the party would down a whisky or two while warming their hands around a pot-bellied stove. Port or sherry was taken outside to the shivering ladies, as it was not thought appropriate for a lady to be seen inside a bar. Were she to enter one, her reputation would suffer irrevocably.

Winter carriages were always strongly in evidence for all the most important occasions in Victoria's history. In 1876, when Lord Dufferin visited the city, the newly operating Winter Carriages was given a boost by an increase in business. Again, in 1882, when the Marquis of Lorne and his wife, Princess Louise, daughter of Queen Victoria, came to Victoria for an extended time, George Winter's carriages were much in demand for all the social events around the city.

When the Native Sons group gave their first formal ball in the Assembly Hall on Fort Street in February 1900, Winter carriages were seen on the streets en masse. All elegantly decorated, the horses pulling the conveyances clip-clopped up and down Fort Street, delivering the elite to the ball. When the festivities finally ended around 3:00 AM, the coachmen roused themselves from a short nap (and perhaps a short nip!), picked up their passengers, and drove them home in style.

Winter Carriages officially operated the livery and hack stable on Fairfield Road in Ross Bay from 1884 onwards, although George Winter was in business for some years prior to that. The property remained in the possession of the Winter family until 1921.

The tradition of operating carriages stayed in the Winter family through the next generation. One of Winter's sons, George junior, became coachman to James Dunsmuir at Burleith. Another son, Robert, was coachman for Judge Paulus Irving. The two brothers often worked together conveying the Dunsmuir and Irving children to school in their one-horse, two-wheeled traps. Later in the day, the Winter brothers would don full livery for a more elegant carriage ride, escorting Mrs. Dunsmuir and Mrs. Irving to their at-home visits around town.

The O'Reilly family also patronized the Winter stables on numerous occasions, and were it not for the coming of the automobile in the early years of the twentieth century, the tradition of Winter carriages might have continued for much longer in Victoria. Young George Winter died of pneumonia in 1909 at age thirty-four, and his father died two years later, shortly after celebrating his seventy-second birthday. His obituary stated that "he was always known for driving the 'very finest on the road.'"[110] By then, the era of the carriage had already passed, marked perhaps by the dawn of the new century.

Victoria had said farewell to the gallant horse, and horseless carriages were now on their way. The very first one, a steam-powered Wolseley, had in fact been seen in BC back in 1899. It was owned by a man in Vancouver, and the *Colonist* reported then that its appearance on the streets merely confirmed that the end was near for the horse-drawn carriage.

Karl Benz of Germany had produced a three-wheeled vehicle in 1885 with the benzine engine placed over the rear axle, following the introduction of the internal combustion engine. Meanwhile, in North America, the first practical car was being built in a barn in Springfield, Massachusetts, in 1892, by Charles E. Duryea, and the Daimler Company had introduced the Panhard car into France by 1894.

Others were also experimenting in the automobile world, including Elwood Hayes, George Selden, and Dave Buick. And, considered by far to be the most amazing, was Henry Ford's first car, a gasoline buggy developed in 1893. It later proved its worth by travelling at a phenomenal twenty miles an hour.

In Victoria, certain forward-thinking gentlemen had watched these world events with interest. It is believed that the first car seen on the streets of the city was brought in by a travelling circus in 1899, but the first automobile of note to be acknowledged as such was owned by Dr. Edward Charles Hart, one-time Victoria coroner. His was a 3.5 horse-power Oldsmobile that arrived in Victoria on May 23, 1902, to be driven down Johnson Street the following day by its proud owner. It set Dr. Hart back nine hundred dollars and was capable of achieving speeds of fifteen miles an hour.

The *Colonist* had stated as early as 1895 that "what with the bicycle and the motor carriage, the horse is indeed becoming obsolete." With the arrival of Dr. Hart's machine, and that of A.E. Todd a year later, the demise of the horse was inevitable.

Albert (Bert) Edward Todd, son of salmon-canning magnate Jacob Hunter Todd and one-time mayor of Victoria, was a fanatic when it came to the automobile. He could hardly wait for his steam-driven car to arrive from San Francisco on the morning of May 26, 1903. Imported to Victoria by inventor Bagster Seabrook, it was built by the White Sewing Machine Company of Cleveland, Ohio.

Accompanied by H.D. Ryus, Todd immediately took his new car on a trial run from Victoria to Shawnigan Lake, logging and timing the whole adventure. The fact that the journey was made without insurance, driver's licence, registration, licence plates, windshield, or fenders was of little consequence. Todd had made history. It was not until the following year that the provincial government introduced licensing with an annual fee of two dollars. The Motor Vehicle Speed Regulation Act then required owners to attach the number of their permit in a conspicuous spot on the back of their vehicle so that it was clearly visible during daylight hours. The licence plates were made of leather.

There were thirty-two licensed car owners on the roads by the end of 1904, and Bert Todd held licence number 13. His dedication and contribution to all road-pioneering pursuits in the early years of the twentieth century earned him titles such as "the father of tourism in British Columbia" and "Good Roads Todd." Certainly his courageous belief in the automobile as something more than a frivolous toy for the rich and privileged had contributed to its eventually becoming a part of everyone's life. He was convinced it would one day shape the economy, geography, and social aspects of the province.

Although he would eventually prove to be right, in the beginning the automobile was little more than a plaything for the very rich, enabling them to jaunt around the countryside in style. Those who wanted to speed (and there were many!) were limited to a reckless ten miles an hour within city limits or fifteen in the country.

The first hundred registrations in Victoria included many members of high society who were eager to join in this latest craze. Most owned a car within the first ten years of the new century.

Mr. and Mrs. H.D. Helmcken, and D.D. McTavish on the
left, with the Helmckens' Pierce Arrow automobile, 1907.

The Butchart family was particularly fond of the automobile. R.P.
Butchart, known as "Leadfoot Bob" because of his tendency to drive at
breakneck speeds, obtained licence number 11 on May 14, 1904. A note
attached later to that registration reads, "Broken Up 8th May 1907." Many
of Butchart's early vehicles met a similar fate.

Jenny Butchart was one of the first women to own a fashionable electric car, which became very popular with the ladies of Victoria. They were
advertised by BC Electric at first as being "clean, safe, simple and economical." Perfect for theatres, weddings, and all social functions, because one
could arrive in immaculate condition, which was, apparently, "so impossible with a gas car."

Bert Todd and sisters out for a drive, c. 1910.
IMAGE (AUTHOR'S COLLECTION) GIVEN TO AUTHOR
BY THE TODD FAMILY FROM THEIR COLLECTION

Elizabeth Rithet was another woman who favoured the electric car. She had a shiny black model with white-spoked wheels. The windows were of beveled plate glass, etched with designs of roses and tulips. The interior of the car contained beautifully upholstered blue velvet seats and sometimes glass vases full of freshly cut flowers. Their presence did not stop Lizzie from driving at high speeds around the streets of Victoria, paying little or no attention to others on the road. Her children claimed that she drove her car with the same wild abandon she always showed when riding her horses.

Just as stables offering hack services had once been big business, so did the business of supplying automobiles become an important part of the town's commercial life. Two enterprising brothers by the name of Hutchison established an "automobile livery" where one could hire vehicles such as a five-passenger White Steamer (with chauffeur) for a fee of four dollars per hour.

By 1906 Cadillacs were also available for hire, and the *Colonist* was carrying advertisements for the amazing "self-starting Winton," a vehicle that enabled its driver to actually start it without leaving his seat. No more back-breaking cranking was necessary, as long as the owner could part with twenty-five hundred dollars to purchase the beast.

J.M. Wood and Thomas Plimley both opened garages in town, and Plimley's became the agent for Humbers and Singers. Plimley even installed a machine at his garage for "restoring the spirits of depressed tires" and announced, "the public are invited to help themselves to wind at Mr. Plimley's expense."[111]

With automobiles becoming more and more popular, the Hutchison brothers reported they would soon be opening a factory to build them in Victoria. Not long after that announcement, an automobile club was formed among the early car owners, with Bert Todd elected as first president. There were soon approximately twenty cars and ten motorcycles on the roads of Victoria, and even the May 24 celebrations were now billed as the "horse and automobile parade."

Many vehicles met an early demise, mainly due to road conditions, which were often atrocious. Intrepid early travellers, including men like Todd, Butchart, Hal Holton, and Dr. Garesche, continued to pursue motoring with increased enthusiasm, and it was their dedication that eventually led to road improvement and Victoria's recognition as a major tourist centre.

By 1910, yet another form of transportation was known in Victoria. William Wallace Gibson made a short and somewhat undignified attempt at notoriety by flying his homemade biplane a short distance and then crashing into a tree on Lansdowne Field in September that year.

No matter the end result, it was just one more indication that the world was getting smaller and the former colony no longer so isolated.

૨૭

"Our house was full of company," wrote Martha Cheney in her journal in September 1853. Her statement was indicative of a lifestyle among the settlers from the very beginning. They liked to entertain and, what is more, they enjoyed writing about it.

Martha Cheney, the young girl who arrived with her aunt and uncle, the Blinkhorns, in 1852, kept a journal peppered with social chit-chat. It is just one of many documents still existing today that enable us to eavesdrop on thoughts, experiences, and conversations in Victoria over a century ago. Although her writing style is sometimes awkward and immature, it does allow the reader to view life as it once was.

"In the afternoon old Mr. Muir came in, and in the evening presently in came John and Archibald Muir. They stayed all night, and then between 9 and 10 o'clock at night, just as we were going to bed, in came Mr. Swanston, Mr. Skinner, Captain Grant and Captain Cooper, . . . a fine houseful [*sic*] some had to go up in the loft to sleep."

Martha also tells of other events. In November 1853 she recalls an earthquake in Victoria. "In the evening we felt a Shock of an Earthquake, which shook the whole house, and which nearly took us off our feet. It was about 5 o'clock."

That same year, "there was a theatre on Board the Man of War *Trincomalee*. Captain and Mrs. Cooper and myself were invited to see the Scene and of course went. Mr. and Mrs. Langford and family, the Governor and his family, and Mr. and Mrs. Skinner, and the Gentlemen from the Fort, went on board about 6 o'clock in the evening."[112]

An indication that despite the isolation of settlers, there was also a fierce determination to maintain a normal social life is seen in Martha's words in March 1854: "Snow, Hail, Rain, and Blowing a hurricane at times all day. [Nonetheless] Mr. and Mrs. Langford, Mrs. Skinner and her babe, Constance Langford Skinner, came over walking from Colwood that miserable day to see us. They were almost Frozen they stayed all night, then went back the next day [which was] fine but very wet." Martha Cheney Ella lived in Metchosin, some distance from the Skinners and Langfords in Esquimalt. In another interesting insight into that Victorian way of life, Martha continues to refer to her new husband as "Mr. Ella" for some time after their marriage. And later, when her husband was sick with dysentery, she describes it in the following words: "After we got him home, we sent for the Doctor, he came next morning, bled him and gave him medicine, kept in bed until the next Thursday, which made him very weak indeed. I was taken very ill myself with the same complaint, was in bed for two days, was very weak."

Letters within the Douglas family are equally enlightening, giving clear insight into the contrasting character traits of James Douglas himself. His overbearing and extremely strict attitude to his only son, James, with constant reprimands on behaviour, educational pursuits, penmanship, and careless habits, is very different from the heartache he expresses when his youngest daughter, Martha, leaves Victoria for schooling and travel in England.

He constantly scolds James with harsh words: "Several of your letters have come to hand, none of them carefully written, either as regards style, orthography or penmanship. They are, in fact, full of blunders, words misspelled, omissions, not of words only, but of whole phrases; errors which a youth of your age ought not to make, and could so easily rectify, were it not for the most inveterate habits of careless indolence which you seem to have fallen into. It is very painful to have such remarks to make on your letters, every time that I write; you appear to have very little regard for my feelings, or you certainly would strive to get rid of these careless habits, which are a perfect torture to me." And concerning his fatherly advice on the subject of marrying too young, he emphasizes his thoughts with the words "Remember this counsel and be wise!"

By contrast, he tells Martha how desolate both he and her mother are after she leaves: "My dearest Martha, I hurried up from the garden gate where I bade you adieu to comfort Mamma—and found her in a burst of uncontrollable grief. I caught her in my arms, but her heart was full. She rushed wildly into her room and, casting herself upon the bed, lay sobbing and calling upon her child. Mamma was at length exhausted, and then I poured in words of consolation, and then drove out to see you pass out of the harbour." Later, "Last night after prayers, in which you were earnestly remembered, Mamma burst into tears and had a good cry; which relieved her feelings, and she was soon all right again."

Waxing somewhat poetic, this often hard man wrote to his daughter of a horseback ride: "I drove out to Rosebank—the woods were charming, fragrant with the perfume of numberless trees and plants and lustrous vernal beauty. Wondrous are the works of God who can show forth His glorious acts."

And perhaps even more surprising, Douglas wrote these words to his youngest daughter: "I have placed a large, beautiful apple on the table in your bedroom. It makes me fancy that you are here—though a mere delusion it alleviates the pain of absence."

The Crease family also takes us on a journey of discovery into the Victorian era. In 1889, daughter Josephine Crease complains about the frequency of social obligations: "we have to go! Bally nuisance."

A few years later, Josephine describes something of the snobbish attitude toward outsiders not considered to be of good family with all the right connections: "Lindley brought a Mr. Hopkins, a complete stranger into dinner," she says. "E. Shrimp, and A. [family members] behaved very shockingly for the stranger's benefit." Not only could the upper class not abide strangers in their midst, they also had very little understanding of or patience with their

Chinese servants. "No Chinaman, left without a word! Oh dear."

And Nellie (Todd) Gillespie, a sister of Bert Todd, remarked: "I remember one very good Chinaman we had. He went off to China and then came back again. My father said, 'Times are very bad now. I can't pay you as much as I did. So the Chinaman came just the same and after a while I said to him, 'Why don't you make those nice little jelly tarts you used to make?' He said, 'Oh, $20 Chinaman not make tarts like that. Only $25 Chinaman make them.'"

Kathleen O'Reilly's words are as vibrant and alive today as they were when first written. When she was eleven years old, she described simple day-to-day activities at Point Ellice House to her father: "The day before yesterday another brood of chickens came out. The hen had her nest somewhere and they are now running about the yard." She writes of visits to "Uncle Joe" (Joseph Trutch) and tells her father: "Jack [her brother] is reading to Mamma who has a headache." Her words to her parents from Tourin, Cappoquin, in County Waterford, Ireland, in 1897 are particularly interesting:

The drawing room was a very pretty sight. The rooms and corridors of the castle are simply beautiful and perfect for entertaining . . . Lord Cudogan is a dear little man . . . I was rather anxious about the ordeal of being presented, and I had so many instructions about curtsying first and then presenting your left cheek for the Lord Lieutenant to kiss and I was told to do it all very slowly as some people get so frightened that they rush first past the dias [*sic*] where all the Vice Regal party are standing. I gave my card to the officer at the Throne Room door who said, 'Curtsy first, won't you?' in a sort of sympathy tone.

Then my name was simply shouted out which was rather disconcerting in itself, but when I got in front of Lord Cudogan, a man in the party said 'The young lady from British Columbia,' and one of the aides performed a sort of war dance! I entirely forgot about the kiss, and His Excellency seized my hand and drew me toward him—they say he never really kisses anyone which is very wise of him I think. Then I made my bow to Her Excellency and passed on. She smiled sweetly.

At the beginning of Kathleen O'Reilly's 1897 diary, she wrote a simple poem. Whether of her own creation or written by someone else and simply enjoyed by her, it helps explain her reluctance to ever trust a man enough to become his wife:

> You call me sweet and tender names,
> And fondly smooth my tresses,
> And all the while my beating heart,
> Keeps time to your caresses.
>
> You love me in your gentle way,
> I answer, as you let me,
> But Oh! There comes another day,
> The day when you'll forget me.

John Andrew Mara, who married Alice Barnard in 1882, also kept interesting diaries. Mara was an adventurous man who had walked across the continent as a member of the famous Overlanders. In his youth he had crossed mountains and battled blizzards, as well as sailing an ocean, and later fought numerous battles in the political arena.

He describes the opening of the new Parliament Buildings in February 1898, a big social event in Victoria. It was apparently "showery and cloudy" that day. "The new Parliament Buildings opened by Lt.-Gov. McInnes at 3 PM. Dr. Helmcken and I occupied seats on the Throne with Mr. Speaker Higgins. There was a big crush and a great deal of confusion. The Chamber looked well, but some of the arrangements were out of place."

Peter O'Reilly's diary that year makes mention of the same occasion: The O'Reillys had "good seats" and the Arion Club performed.

A later diary of Mara's describes a meeting he had with Peter O'Reilly in London soon after the death of Caroline O'Reilly: "Saw O'Reilly and Frank at the Euston Hotel—the former is terribly cut up over the death of his wife."

Peter O'Reilly's grief seemed to be the topic of many conversations. Even Lady Macdonald, in her continued correspondence with the O'Reillys after her visit to Victoria, remarks to Kathleen: "he looked so sad and changed after his grievous sorrow that all who met him were distressed—those especially who know what he had lost in your dear mother."

Meanwhile, Mara's diaries also give a glimpse into the travels abroad of a typical upper-class family. In 1900, John Mara, Alice, and their two children, Nellie and Lytton, travelled to London, primarily to settle Nellie into school there. They also took time to do a little sightseeing in London. "In the afternoon, we went to the Albert Hall Concert. The size of the Hall and the large attendance was a surprise to Nellie ... We saw the Horse Guards changing ... [and] then took Nellie to the Art Gallery." They also visited the Monument and London Bridge and were particularly impressed with St. Paul's. A visit out of London to Oxfordshire took them to Blenheim "to see the Meet ... Alice and the children had never seen a Meet before."

In February, the Mara family attended *Puss in Boots* at the Garrick Theatre, and they also took time for some shopping. An umbrella at Dickins & Jones cost Mara one pound two shillings and sixpence, whereas his golf suit from Hope Brothers cost him three pounds nine shillings and sixpence. In addition, the family frequently visited the Army & Navy Store for wool shirts and socks. With his political interests, Mara went to the House of Lords to sit in on debates, and was ever conscious of the happenings in South Africa as news of the war reached London on a daily basis.

George Winter Carriage outside Cary Castle, George senior on left.
IMAGE B-00472 COURTESY OF ROYAL BC MUSEUM, BC ARCHIVES

"Good news from South Africa," Mara announced on February 18, 1900. Then on March 1, "News of the relief of Ladysmith received at 10 a.m . . . The whole of London frantic with joy. Business in the city practically suspended. All traffic stopped in the vicinity of the Mansion House."

Clearly, the early residents of Victoria, with their connections and interests around the world, were far from isolated despite living, as they did, on the far side of the Rockies. Their pasts and their continued interest in travel, plus their regular correspondence with friends and relatives around the world, kept them abreast of the times and in touch with world affairs.

(The quotes in the conversations section of this chapter come from the following sources: the Diary of Martha Cheney Ellis, the Douglas Correspondence, the Crease Correspondence, the O'Reilly Collection, the article by Willard Ireland on Walter Grant, and the Diary of John A. Mara, which are all provided in the bibliography.)

# CHAPTER ELEVEN

# *Residences, Rituals, and Rites*

Dressing in silk, satin, or expensive brocade, and driving in highly polished, liveried carriages or the very latest electric automobile were mere trimmings to a life of overall wealth and elegance. For those who liked to think of themselves as Victoria's elite, a more accurate symbol of their financial status was their homes.

From the beginning, it had been of paramount importance to be a person of property, and the grander and more elegant that property was, the more superior its owner felt.

The homes in this chapter are a sample of that earnestly sought-after splendour, a splendour that existed even in the days when Amelia Douglas longed to escape the confines of the fort and set up her own home. It continued down through the years, gaining momentum with every new home built in Victoria, as each attempted to out-do the one that went before.

A certain elite way of life was reflected by those homes. It is interesting to note, however, that of the sixteen residences and mansions mentioned here, only seven remain, an indication that the era when such regal mansions reigned supreme was short-lived.

☙

Mullachard—home of the first colonist in Sooke.
IMAGE PDP34 COURTESY OF ROYAL BC MUSEUM, BC ARCHIVES

In 1849, some twenty-five miles from Fort Victoria in the wild Sooke countryside, Vancouver Island's first settler, Captain Walter Colquhoun Grant, set about the unenviable task of clearing the land on which he proposed to settle.

The location, though truly isolated, seemed ideal as it was suitable for a sawmill as well as a house and the necessary farm buildings. The house was originally called Achaineach, but more commonly referred to as Mullachard, and was built of square logs, roofed with cedar shakes. It was located in the Sooke Harbour area between two rocky knolls on which were mounted two cannon.[113] Grant also built adjacent accommodation for his labourers, adequate farm buildings, and the sawmill, and then set about cultivating at least thirty-five acres of his one hundred.

Grant's dreams for future expansion on the adjacent one hundred acres, in order to form a small Scottish colony, never materialized.

Douglas home on Elliot Street.
IMAGE CVA 98303-07-451

James and Amelia Douglas's house, built in 1851, stood a little to the east of Government Street between Belleville and Elliot streets, near where the Royal British Columbia Museum stands today. It faced south and was surrounded by a fine garden. The grounds sloped down to the water's edge. Although given authority to build another house as an official government residence, Douglas preferred to use his own home for all official occasions.

Building a large mansion in those early days was a problem. With no contractors and numerous difficulties in obtaining materials, construction was a slow process. The Douglas home was a Quebecois-style house, rectangular with two storeys and an attic. Divided by a wide hall, the main floor consisted of dining room and kitchen, and a front and back drawing room. Upstairs there were three bedrooms and another wide hall.

An 1861 assessment roll shows that the land was valued at four thousand pounds and improvements at ten thousand, nine hundred and fifty pounds. The following year the land was assessed at thirty-eight thousand pounds, but in 1868, after Douglas had subdivided the property, it was assessed at only six thousand, five hundred pounds with improvements at two thousand pounds.[114]

Amelia Douglas continued to live in the house for thirteen years after her husband died, seldom leaving the estate until her own death in January 1890. Members of the family lived on there for another decade. In 1902, an auction was held at what was billed as "the Old Colonial Official Residence." At that time, most of the Douglas furniture was sold. On October 4, 1906, the house itself was sold by auction and then demolished in order to allow Elliot Street to go through to Government.

Only the cherry tree in James Douglas's garden continues to bloom to this day as a reminder of the old Douglas home.

☙

Helmcken House, the second-oldest house in the province, was built in 1853 for the young fort doctor, James Helmcken, and his bride, Cecilia Douglas, on property adjacent to the Douglas house. The contractor was Gideon Halcrow.

In view of shortages of both labour and material, it was no easy matter to build a house at that time. Helmcken himself stated in his *Reminiscences* that

> there being no lumber, it had to be built with logs squared on two sides and six inches thick. The sills and uprights were very heavy and morticed—the supports of the floor likewise—the logs had to be let into grooves in the uprights.
>
> Well, the timber had to be taken from the forest—squared there and brought down by water. All this had to be contracted for by French

Home of Dr. James Helmcken—638 Elliot Street.
IMAGE CVA 98303-07-318

Canadians, then when brought to the beach—I had to beg big oxen of the company to haul it to the site. Then other Canadians took the job of putting the building up as far as the logs were concerned—and then shingling—the Indians at this time made shingles—all split. All this was very heavy, very expensive, and very slow work, for the men were by no means in a hurry . . .

Well, the shell is up—now to get it finished—lumber very scarce and a favour to get any at forty dollars per thousand in the rough—so it all had to be planed and grooved by hand! Much of it was cut by Kanakas in a saw pit—so it was not very regular thickness. He [presumably Halcrow the contractor] had a yellow cedar planking for doors, windows, and skirting boards sent down to him from Fort Rupert.[115]

It is a testament to the soundness of the building, however, that Helmcken House still stands on its original site, over a hundred and fifty years later. Today, the pioneer doctor's residence (the oldest house in the province open to the public) also has an incredible medical collection on display and is open from mid-June to mid-September (10:00 AM to 5:00 PM) with special holiday events offered at other times of the year, catering to school or other special groups.

☙

Overlooking Esquimalt Harbour, later to be known as Skinner's Cove, Oaklands was built in 1853, high up on a sunny slope. Many oak trees had to be cleared to accommodate the twin-gabled, one-storey structure for the growing Skinner family. The house was apparently "solidly built, homelike, and charming. Its shuttered windows opened wide to the fresh air and sunshine."[116]

Mary Skinner planted a large garden around her home, reminiscent of the one she had left behind in England. It was full of all her favourite English flowers and enclosed by a trellis fence, giving all who came upon it the feeling they had discovered an oasis of beauty in that early colonial wilderness.

Oaklands has long since disappeared, and today Skinner's Cove is the location of the Esquimalt Graving Dock.

The original J.D. Pemberton home was built in the late 1850s by men of the Hudson's Bay Company. At that time, Pemberton paid them forty pounds to build him a thirty- by-twenty-foot log house with a barn and some outbuildings. The cabin was surrounded by five cultivated acres.

Oaklands—the Skinners' residence.
IMAGE B-00179 COURTESY OF ROYAL BC MUSEUM, BC ARCHIVES

In that small place, Pemberton and his sister managed, by candlelight, to entertain many of the early colonists. The old traditions of dressing for dinner, and a dining table with white tablecloth, china, sparkling glassware, and good wine, were carried on as though the cabin were an elegant mansion in London.

After Pemberton's marriage, and with subsequent years of accumulating wealth and acreage, he was able, in 1885, to build Gonzales, a fine type of English country home, at Rockland and St. Charles.

Gonzales was little short of palatial. Its massive ten thousand square feet contained twenty rooms. The drawing room was an enormous forty-five feet by eighteen feet, and the dining room thirty feet by eighteen. There were five bathrooms, a billiard room, a library, and a separate writing

Gonzales—home of the Pemberton family.
IMAGE A-07779 COURTESY OF ROYAL BC MUSEUM, BC ARCHIVES

room. The tower held a conservatory with splendid views of the city and the ocean. All the rooms were so large and high ceilinged, and so difficult to heat, that dinner guests often complained of shivering throughout the entire evening.

Following Teresa Pemberton's death in 1916, the Gonzales estate was broken up, but the children continued to live on parts of the property. The house itself was sold and for a number of years was used as the residence of Norfolk House Girls School. Until the 1930s some of the roads in the area, such as Gonzales between Despard Avenue and Foul Bay Road, which once formed the original driveway, were still private property. In November 1952, Gonzales was demolished. The demolition crew was said to have found five gallons of honey in hives between the walls of the once elegant mansion.

Mount Joy—Fred Pemberton's home.
IMAGE CVA 98303-01-601

Mount Joy once stood at the corner of Foul Bay and Fairfield roads and was the home of Frederick Bernard Pemberton, J.D. Pemberton's eldest son. The house was named for Mountjoy Square in Dublin, where Fred Pemberton's great-grandfather, the mayor of Dublin, had once lived; it was built in 1903 on ten acres that were part of the original Gonzales estate. Mount Joy was known for is thirteen tiled fireplaces and a conservatory with its own miraculous heating plant. Fred Pemberton died in November 1947 at the age of eighty-three, and the house was subsequently sold. It sat vacant until March 1953, at which time it burned to the ground in a spectacular fire.

Today, Pentrelew Place, heading south from Fort Street near the Art Gallery of Greater Victoria, marks the spot where once the estate of Henry Pering Pellew Crease was located.

Pentrelew—home of the Crease family.
IMAGE CVA 98407-25-537

Pentrelew itself was built in 1875 on property Crease had acquired in the early 1870s. His intention had been to build a house in what was then the fashionable Italianate style, similar to Queen Victoria's Osborne House on the Isle of Wight. He wrote to Wright and Sanders, San Francisco architects, regarding the design of the home, and he had very definite ideas. "We want the house plain but pleasing with clear bold projections and good exterior."[117] Both Henry and his wife, Sarah, made numerous suggestions in their correspondence and obviously wanted them all incorporated into the final design of Pentrelew.

The name Pentrelew was taken from the Cornish word meaning "house-on-land-sloping-two-ways." It was originally quite modest, but in 1890 was enlarged considerably. Additions to the house were designed by Leonard Buttress Trimen and included a three-storey, campanile-style tower, dormer windows, and many more rooms. Eventually, the house contained eleven bedrooms, two drawing rooms, a very large dining room, two pantries, a study, a morning room, and two kitchens.

Pentrelew soon became the site for important, high-society entertaining and often overflowed with guests from around the world. The large grounds surrounding the house were also famous for many years, the scenes of picnics and summer entertainments. It was said that hardly an admiral in the British navy had not, as a midshipman, once climbed the cherry trees at Pentrelew.

The English oaks behind the house are supposed to have been grown from acorns Henry Crease received from the English jurist Torrens, who had collected them from beneath the Tree of Liberty in the garden of William Pitt the Younger (under which tree, William Wilberforce, the renowned emancipator, had made a pledge to free slaves around the world).

Some more modern amenities such as electric light did not come to Pentrelew until the late 1930s. The house itself survived at 1201 Fort Street as the Victoria Truth Centre for some years but was much altered from its original design. Finally, in 1984, it was demolished.

ᔆ

Ince was built for Arthur Crease and his wife, the former Helen Tyrwhitt-Drake, daughter of a well-known Victoria judge, in 1908. The couple had married in 1903 and first lived in James Bay at the corner of Superior Street and Bird Cage Walk (which is today Government Street). In 1908 they commissioned architect William Ridgeway Wilson to design a larger home for them, and Ince was the result. The style was definite Tudor Revival, with its half-timbering on the upper storey and large columns next to the lower windows. Eight fireplaces were installed in the mansion.

In the 1950s, Ince was converted to suites. It still stands today at 2021 McNeill Avenue and is an important heritage asset, the last reminder of that once-famous legal family.

Ince—2021 McNeill (Arthur Crease's home).
IMAGE F-07701 COURTESY OF ROYAL BC MUSEUM, BC ARCHIVES

♥◑

Point Ellice House at 2616 Pleasant Street is one of Victoria's oldest houses. Built by John Work around 1861 for his daughter, Kate, and son-in-law, Charles Wentworth Wallace, a steamboat and mining man, it has had a number of alterations through the years.

In 1867, Peter O'Reilly bought the house for fourteen thousand dollars and moved in with his family. He and Caroline raised their children there (their daughter Kathleen being born only a matter of weeks after they moved in). They also entertained many important guests in the house, including the first prime minister of Canada, Sir John A. Macdonald.

The house has twelve rooms and seven fireplaces, and the kitchen has a built-in French range and a brick inside chimney. Architects John Teague and William Ridgeway Wilson designed some of the alterations to the house at various times. Many of the original interior furnishings still exist today, including Persian rugs and much of the O'Reillys' furniture. Members of the O'Reilly family lived at Point Ellice until the 1960s, when they opened the single-storey home to the public as a museum.

This private enterprise did not succeed, so in December 1974, the provincial government purchased Point Ellice House with all its contents and also opened it as a tourist attraction. Through the years since then, it has become a well-known historic site in Victoria and, like Helmcken House, is open for viewing from mid-June to mid-September, with daily tours of the house and garden—a garden that is a magnificent example of Victoriana in all its original splendour.

**☙**

Fairfield House on Trutch Street was once approached by a long driveway, which now is part of Collinson Street. It was an elegant home and, according to the historian J.K. Nesbitt's "Old Homes & Families," was situated in acres of grounds . . . [with] oldtimers remembering 'the Trutch estate' as it was called, for its fields painted purple and gold and lily white with wild flowers. Horses grazed under the trees and cows chewed in the pastures, which are today the streets and houses of the Fairfield neighbourhood.

The exact date of the house's construction is not clear, but it was around 1861 when Joseph Trutch purchased ten acres of land (formerly part of Governor James Douglas's Fairfield Farm) and there built what was described as a prettily situated, modest cottage. In 1864, Trutch lent his house to Governor Kennedy for use as the vice-regal mansion while Cary Castle was undergoing renovations.

Point Ellice House (home of the O'Reillys), c. 1903.
IMAGE CVA 98303-0604373

The year after Trutch's death, the Trutch estate was subdivided and Trutch Street was put through. In 1906, the *Colonist* bemoaned this march of progress:

Tis goodbye to the estate where broom was first planted in Victoria—one by one the family demesnes—the scenes of old-time gaieties—are being swept away by the growth of the city and now the historic Trutch homestead is being divided up in the march of commercialism ... The library, with its bookshelves in alcoves on either side of the open fireplace, and the drawing room, recall the many festivities held in the old mansion, when crinolined belles stepped gracefully through quadrilles and minuets, but abhorred that new fangled invention, the waltz."[118]

Another writer remarked that there were many traces of its elegant past. The gracefully turned banister is Spanish mahogany. At the bend in the

Fairfield House on Trutch Street.
IMAGE C-01218 COURTESY OF ROYAL BC MUSEUM, BC ARCHIVES

staircase is a magnificent stained-glass window, with green, red, and purple lights like emeralds, rubies, and amethysts. The fireplace mantel in the former library is California redwood, and in some rooms six-inch flooring still sparkles and shines. There are eight fireplaces, twenty-eight doors, and thirty-six windows. The high gables and eaves are typical of the times in which the house was built. Its low windows looked across the gardens and fields to the hills of Sooke, and it was said there was no finer sunset view in all Victoria than from the paved terrace that skirted the outside of Fairfield House.[119]

Interestingly, Trutch himself did not gain legal title to his home until 1890, well after the death of James Douglas. Trutch had previously only rented the land from the Douglas estate.

After the property was subdivided, the house lost some of its value. Through the years, many other families lived at Fairfield House, including the Springetts and the Fatts. The house's name was changed to

Hollybank—952 Humboldt Street (the Rithets' home), c. 1903.
IMAGE CVA 98303-06-4378

Dulce Domun and later to Villa Elenore when it became a guest house. Renovations in the 1980s have now made the old home of Joseph and Julia Trutch an important part of the Trutch Street cluster of character houses.

Hollybank, which once stood at 952 Humboldt Street, was east of the site of the Fairfield Health Centre (the old St. Joseph's Hospital). The Rithet family owned the entire block bounded by Humboldt, Vancouver, Collinson, and Quadra streets.

The house was built as a wedding gift for Robert Rithet and his bride, the former Elizabeth Munro, by her father, Alexander Munro, a retired Hudson's Bay Company factor. The young couple moved in soon after their wedding in 1875.

Hollybank was once one of the most beautiful and elegant mansions in Victoria. It was especially noted for its iron fence, six chimneys, holly trees,

The Beaconsfield—998 Humboldt (Genge family home), c. 1959.
IMAGE CVA 98202-19-1191

and winding garden paths. To the rear of the property was a two-storey barn with a number of outbuildings. In the paddocks numerous horses roamed.

The Rithet family remained at Hollybank for many years. The house was finally demolished in 1953 shortly after Elizabeth Rithet's death, but a piece of the famous iron railing fence was saved and moved to the grounds of the Royal British Columbia Museum. Today it surrounds James Douglas's cherry tree, planted there in 1854.

In keeping with tradition, Robert Rithet also presented *his* daughter with a house as a wedding gift when she married Lawrence Genge in 1904. The

Genge house, at 998 Humboldt, was built at the eastern end of the Rithet property. It was a Maclure design and underwent more Maclure renovations in 1913.

Hip-roofed and shingle-clad with a half-timbered second floor, the original design had a veranda on one side and an entrance porch on the other. The 1913 renovation added a sunroom gallery across the entire front elevation at ground-floor level. The house still exists as a bed and breakfast, called The Beaconsfield.

୧୬

Duvals, at 1462 Rockland Avenue, was built around 1860 for Mrs. Elizabeth Miles, who later bought Cary Castle and sold it to Governor Arthur Kennedy. Duvals was later owned by Chief Justice Joseph Needham, who sold it to Francis J. Barnard in 1870. In 1895, his son, Harry Barnard, took his new bride to Duvals, and they lived there for the rest of their lives.

The home remained in the Barnard family for nearly eighty-five years, during which time it was the scene of many social functions. Today it is known as the Mary Manor Apartments on Rockland Avenue, opposite Government House.

୧୬

The original Clovelly, built by A.J. Weaver, burned down and was rebuilt in 1894. At that time it was the residence of Mrs. A.J.W. Bridgman, and a *Colonist* report that year described the house:

> Scarcely ever before, even in the brightest times, have so many houses of
> the first-class sprung into life in one year as in this year of Our Lord, 1894.
> One is in Esquimalt, the residence of Mrs. A.J.W. Bridgman. The principal

Duvals on Rockland Avenue (the Barnards' home).
IMAGE CVA 98108-12-2720 120

feature is the beauty of the cedar panelling in the hall and inglenook, the drawing room being entirely of this exquisite wood. Another point of merit is the massive cedar staircase with the lower newel running to the ceiling and with a double arch on either side, through which is seen the 24-light stained-glass window. It would be hard to find a home which, though by no means large, is so complete in every respect. The contractor for the whole is Mr. George McFarland.[120]

In 1908 the house was sold to Sir Francis S. Barnard and his wife, and called Clovelly by them. It soon became the elegant backdrop for Lady Barnard's numerous dinner parties, which earned fame due to their delicious menus, exquisite dining ambience, and guests from the upper echelon of society.

Clovelly in Esquimalt (home of Sir Frank Barnard).
IMAGE CVA 98308-03-3498

By 1949, Clovelly, at 761 Sea Terrace, was occupied by the Sisters of the Love of Jesus. It was demolished in 1960.

The present-day Government House on Rockland Avenue, official residence for the lieutenant-governors of BC, is the third building to occupy that site. Today it is surrounded by nearly thirty acres of gardens. The previous two government residences both met the same fate, destruction by fire—the first in 1899 and the second in 1957.

Government House was long called simply Cary Castle. It was named for the original builder and first occupant, George Hunter Cary, who built

Government House/Cary Castle, residence of the lieutenant Governor of BC, c. 1910.
IMAGE CVA #8

his somewhat unusual, castle-like, turret home on a hillside overlooking Ross Bay in the early 1860s. Upon returning to England, Cary had left his castle vacant. It was bought by Mrs. Elizabeth Miles, who named it Stoneleigh.

When the new governor, Arthur Kennedy, arrived in Victoria in 1864, there was no official residence for him, and he purchased Cary Castle from Mrs. Miles. Kennedy did substantial renovation work before finally moving himself and his family into the house in July 1865. He spent a great deal of money in the process and was criticized for his extravagance.

Subsequent lieutenant-governors made other alterations to the castle until the original was hardly recognizable. Julia Trutch, during her husband's tenure there, brought larks and other songbirds from England, and tried to recreate a pleasant environment for them in the gardens.

One of the many important personages who stayed at the official residence (and also fell in love with it despite criticism from others) was

Princess Louise, Queen Victoria's daughter. During her three-month stay there, she described it as "halfway between heaven and Balmoral."

The original Cary Castle burned to the ground on May 18, 1899, and the then lieutenant-governor, Thomas Mcinnes, was said to have escaped with only the clothes on his back. The A.A. Green residence, known as Gyppeswyck, became the official government residence for a while at a monthly rent of fifty dollars, until another Government House could be built. By the middle of 1903, the new Government House was ready for occupancy. There was also a new lieutenant-governor, Sir Henri-Gustave Joly de Lotbinière.

James Dunsmuir succeeded de Lotbinière in 1906 and brought a new meaning to the words elegance, wealth, and entertainment. His American-born wife was an excellent hostess whose entertainment extravaganzas had never been seen in Victoria. The large Dunsmuir family (two sons and eight daughters) meant more additions to the house, including a nursery.

Through the coming years, there were constant fears and numerous warnings about the possibility of another fire, because of defective wiring and cigar and cigarette burns to rugs. An additional threat was the possibility of a brush fire in the surrounding grounds. On April 15, 1957, predictions came true and a "blast-like fire wiped out BC's historic Government House" once again, said the *Colonist*.

[T]all, fire-blackened chimneys and an ornamental battlement rise today above the ashes and charred debris of what was once Government House ... Stately rooms that were never coldly impersonal, that were always blessed with a warm, human graciousness, have gone ... Through the massive oak doors had walked men and women of all degrees, received with a hospitality that brought stature to the province and had won respect, admiration and affection for those who dispensed it.[121]

New plans were soon under way for the third official Government House, with the final design reflecting the Maclure and Rattenbury style and incorporating the old stone porte cochère and tower left standing after the fire. Costs, not including furnishings, were estimated to be eight hundred thousand dollars.

Excavation for the new residence began in December; meanwhile, the flag of the lieutenant-governor flew over the Empress Hotel throughout the 1958 centennial celebrations. Princess Margaret and her large entourage stayed in the vice-regal suite at the Empress. On April 26, 1959, Lieutenant-Governor Ross moved into the new mansion, and in subsequent years numerous royal visitors and other notable guests have passed through the doors. A scroll bearing the word "Salve" (Latin for "welcome") is engraved in the drawing room's marble fireplace.

Today, the exquisite grounds of Government House, where a volunteer gardener program is now in place, are frequently used as a setting for wedding parties.

కొ

William John Macdonald, who came to Victoria from Scotland in 1851 working for the Hudson's Bay Company, later prospered so well in business that he was able to purchase twenty-eight acres of prime real estate in James Bay.

In 1876, he commissioned architect Thomas Trounce to design a home for him. The result, a two-storey stone-and-brick residence completed in 1877, could only be described as imposing. It was built in the style of a castle on Skye and called Armadale.

Armadale had ten rooms on the ground floor and another twelve upstairs. The thirty-three-foot-long drawing room had a twelve-foot ceiling. The main staircase was polished mahogany. Eight solid marble

Armadale (Macdonald residence), c. 1903.
IMAGE CVA 98303-06

fireplaces graced the residence, as did embossed ceilings and gold-and-black wallpaper. The house was naturally the scene of many an important social function, as it lent itself admirably to entertaining. Among its distinguished guests were Princess Louise, and Prime Minister Sir John A. Macdonald.

The grounds of Armadale contained stables and a carriage house, as well as rolling lawns, tennis courts, and bridle paths, all adding to its beauty. William Macdonald and his wife, the former Catherine Balfour Reid, raised their six children (three sons and three daughters) at Armadale. During their absence abroad from 1890 until 1892, the house was rented to the Beetons. Henry Coppinger Beeton was a partner in the firm of Turner, Beeton and Company, wholesalers at the time of the Klondike gold rush. Beeton was also agent general for BC in London for a while. When he himself retired from public life, he moved to Weston-super-Mare in England and called his own house there Armadale.

In 1913, two years before Senator William Macdonald died, a syndicate of British and Canadian businessmen made him a substantial offer for his Armadale estate for a future housing development. In the spring of 1914, the senator and his unmarried daughter, Lilias, moved to Oak Bay, where William worked on his memoirs.

The land surrounding Armadale was subdivided into building lots, but a slump in the real estate market caused the whole deal to fall through, and the property reverted back to Macdonald for a while. Later it went to the city. The part south of Niagara Street became residential property while land to the north formed Macdonald Park. William Macdonald donated a portion of the land to be reserved as a playground. Niagara Street today cuts through what was once the driveway to Armadale.

Armadale itself was later converted into apartments. During the Second World War it also served as a nightclub, but because of the need for extensive repair, it slowly fell victim to neglect and vandalism. It was finally demolished in 1949, despite efforts to save the historic landmark.

Within the walls of the aforementioned mansions, one of Victoria's favourite rituals took place on a regular basis: the all-important tea time.

In the early years of Queen Victoria's reign, tea had simply meant the practice of drinking cups of tea. Less than thirty years later, it had taken on a whole new meaning. It was now referred to as tea time or high tea and had become not only an additional meal but a veritable tradition among those of British descent.

The whole phenomenon can perhaps be attributed to actress Fanny Kemble's visit to the Duke of Rutland's castle at Belvoir, where one of her fellow guests was Anna, Duchess of Bedford.

Princess Louise, daughter of Queen Victoria.

I received on several occasions private and rather mysterious invitations to the Duchess of Bedford's room and found her with a "small and select" circle of female guests, busily employed in brewing and drinking tea, with her grace's own private tea-kettle. I do not believe that now universally honoured and observed institution of "five o'clock tea" dates farther back in the annals of English civilization than this very private and, I think, rather shamefaced, practice of it.[122]

With every passing year, more and more food was consumed with the beverage—including thin bread and butter, biscuits, cakes, muffins, hot scones, delicate watercress or cucumber sandwiches, and assorted buns and shortbreads—until finally the ritual had turned into a rather splendid tradition of special treats. Originally meant merely to alleviate the Duchess of Bedford's "sinking feeling" while waiting for dinner at 8:00 PM, it could now be classified as a meal on its own.

Tea time arrived in Victoria with the upper-class ladies from England, all of whom prided themselves upon their teas. Their importance in society was very often judged by the standard of their teas, and they continued the tradition at their weekly at-homes well into the twentieth century.

By the turn of that century, Victoria was also well known for the many tea rooms scattered around the city. The Zetland, the Tea Kettle, Clays, the Cozy Corner, and Spencer's tea rooms were all well patronized by the residents. In addition, most of the best hotel dining rooms, such as those at the Dallas and the Driard, served tea at 4:00 PM every day.

The Driard was once considered to be as fashionable and as grand as the rather splendid Palace Hotel in San Francisco, and was described in Emily Carr's words as "all red plush and palm trees." Having tea there was thought to be the very last word in elegance.

Another equally important ritual in early Victoria was the garden party. Each high-society family tried to outdo the others with the splendour of their grounds and the extravagance of their parties. Some of the grandest were held by the O'Reillys at Point Ellice House on the Gorge. Many famous people disembarked from a barge at the O'Reilly boathouse and strode up the gravel path to the rolling green lawns to enjoy a game of croquet (another ritual) or a set of tennis, or simply to sip tea in elegant surroundings. Those lawns also hosted the first women's provincial tennis championships.

The O'Reilly gardens were renowned for their beauty. This was hardly surprising, as the O'Reilly family members were all avid gardeners and prided themselves on their horticultural talents. Gardening was considered by them, and by most of the elite, to be both spiritually and morally uplifting.

Kathleen O'Reilly carried on the gardening tradition after her father's death in 1905. Hollyhocks, roses, jasmine, lily, and lilac are just a few of the delights to be found in this lovely old-world garden, where once the upper class in Victoria carried on the tradition of garden parties of the finest kind.

The O'Reillys kept extensive records in their diaries and journals of the laying out and planting schedules of their gardens, and they retained many seed catalogues and receipts. This has enabled historians to restore the gardens to the original concept for, by the 1950s, the gardens had become completely overgrown. Restoration was a mammoth undertaking, but it has been ongoing since the mid-1980s. Treasures such as the redwood tree planted by O'Reilly in 1876, as part of the woodland walk to protect his garden from prevailing winds and to provide a cool place to walk on a hot day, still exist.

Another important place to be invited for a croquet party was the Bowker family residence in Oak Bay. John Sylvester Bowker, an American, had come to British Columbia in the 1850s to try his luck in the Cariboo. He then farmed for a while on San Juan Island, and from there he frequently took his boat over to Oak Bay to call on his old friend, Hudson's

Bay Company man John Tod. In May 1864, Bowker married Tod's daughter, Mary, and the couple spent their time between their sheep farm on San Juan Island and the Tod acreage in Oak Bay. Mary Bowker later became a renowned hostess at the Oak Bay farm. The setting was perfect for croquet lawns; some said they were the finest in the northwest, as they stretched almost to the beach at Willows and faced the islands across the strait. There was a tea house on the lawns and tea was served under the trees. Some guests even donned bathing suIts for a swim, thereby initiating the now-popular Willows Beach.

Another important ritual was the wedding ceremony and reception that, through the years, became a status symbol for the wealthy, as it depicted their standing in the community.

Two of the first and certainly the most charming wedding descriptions can be found in the words of Dr. James Helmcken and Martha Cheney. Both were simple affairs. That did not last, however, and it soon became popular to hold weddings of a very grand nature.

In the beginning, life was uncomplicated. When Helmcken married Cecilia Douglas at Christmas in 1852, he describes the nuptials in the following amusing manner:

The day before the time fixed it snowed and it snowed—lord, how it snowed!—so that a couple of feet of snow lay on the ground. The only thing approaching to a carriage was a two-wheeled light cart—the governor's carriage—useless, there not being any roads. The bridegroom (himself) goes to church. The bride (his intended) and her maidens at home, waiting for the carriage. The cart was at the fort, had travelled a hundred yards the wheels no longer would turn and there was a dead stop. The charioteer, a lively, active, good-natured French-Canadian gentleman, full of resource, got an idea. He sent to the store for a dry-goods box, cut off the top and one side, put a seat in and threw some scarlet cloth over all.

Having hewn a couple of willows growing close at hand, of these he made shaft and runners all in one! The box arriving is fixed upon the willow runners, the horse harnessed, the sleigh hastens for the bride and maids.

The poor bridegroom is waiting impatiently in the mess-room church; the hour approaches twelve! His best man rushes into the mess-room, to put the clock hands back, when he suddenly encounters the chaplain's wife, dismayed he kicks out a dog, to disguise his intentions, and returns disappointed. The chaplain appears, and says, if the bride does not arrive before twelve, it only wants a quarter now, I will not be able to perform the ceremony today, it being illegal to do so. Here's a pretty kettle of fish; but just then the tinkle of the sleigh bells are heard, and the bridesmaids and dry-goods box appear. The whole party hurry into the church, the ceremony is proceeding, the clock strikes twelve, just as the ring is put on the finger, etc.: the ceremony over, the bride and bridegroom leave the church to return to their parents' house for a good time, and then the guns roar from the bastions. The bell in the middle of the fort rings—the dogs howl thereunder—the men fire muskets—all hurrah. Grog is served out all round, there is feasting, revelling and jollity, and everybody heart and soul wishes the handsome, favorite, and favored couple very many happy new years.[123]

This was a lesson in ingenuity; the old maxim "to improvise is to specialize" came to the fore.

Martha Cheney describes her wedding to Captain Ella on July 16, 1855, in an equally delightful manner:

I was married to Mr. Ella by the Rev. Mr. Cridge. We were married at home by special licence. It was a beautiful day, but very warm; we had a large dinner party, had a tent made out of doors, it being too warm in the house for so many people. The governor and his family honoured us with their company.[124]

In England in April 1853, another wedding showed the beginning of a trend toward the grander and more extravagant nuptials seen in Victoria in later years. Henry Crease married Sarah Lindley at Acton Church in London, and the apparel of bride, groom, and bridesmaids was of the utmost importance. In addition, the wedding cake was described as "a magnificent one, it stood 2 feet high with the ornaments."[125] The Creases' honeymoon is even mentioned: it was spent on the Isle of Wight.

An important wedding, which was also an interesting alliance from a political standpoint, took place between Constance Skinner and Alexander Davie in 1874. The ceremony was held at the Skinners' Cowichan home, Farleigh, and was presided over by the Reverend David Holmes.

Two of the O'Reilly family weddings were also social events of note. Caroline Trutch and Peter O'Reilly's wedding in 1863 was a fairy-tale event. The sun shone brightly on that December day and the trees were festooned with glistening snow, as the carriage in which Caroline rode to Christ Church Cathedral with her brother set off on its journey. The carriage was decked with ribbons and rosettes and afterward carried the bride and groom to a wedding breakfast at Fairfield House. The honeymoon was spent at Belmont.

When their son, Arthur John O'Reilly, married Mary Beresford Windham, the wedding party was dressed in outfits that were fashionably rich, and the honeymoon was spent in Paris.

A Pemberton wedding of note took place between Ada Georgina Pemberton, J.D. Pemberton's eldest daughter, and Hugo Robert Beaven in 1905. The ceremony was performed by the Right Reverend Bishop Cridge, who also proposed the health of the couple at the reception. He reminded the couple and their guests that

on such occasions there must be room not only for mirth, but for those hallowed memories which may keep their place in our hearts. The wheel of life must move, but our hearts are none the less tender, because we take the cup of joy, as we take the cup of sorrow, knowing both are from the hand of God.[126]

An interesting collection of gifts at the Pemberton wedding is mentioned, including an onyx clock and candelabra from the manager and staff of the Canadian Bank of Commerce, and a set of silver cruets from the staff of Pemberton & Son.

In a popular, quaintly worded phrase of the times, "a marriage was arranged and did take place" between John Trutch and Zoe Musgrave in December 1871. Here again, celebrations were elaborate, and the reception afterward was held at Cary Castle. As Zoe was the sister of the last royal governor, His Excellency Anthony Musgrave, as well as the future sister-in-law of the first lieutenant-governor, Joseph Trutch, the choice of Government House for the reception was appropriate.

The wedding in 1904 between Lawrence Genge and Gertrude Rithet was perhaps the very last word in splendour. Both Christ Church Cathedral, where the ceremony was performed by the Venerable Archdeacon Scriven, and Hollybank, where the wedding reception took place, were decorated with a brilliant profusion of flowers. The grounds of Hollybank were festooned with coloured lanterns, and everyone agreed the setting was perfect. Other than the Dunsmuir wedding extravaganzas, few families could compete with the Genge-Rithet wedding that year.

In 1882, when Alice Barnard married John Andrew Mara, the guests gathered at Duvals to witness the ceremony, performed in the drawing room by the Reverend Stephen. Later in the evening, furniture and carpets were cleared away and dancing went on well into the night, followed by a sumptuous meal at midnight.

The following year, Alice's brother Frank married Martha Loewen at the Loewen home on Pandora Avenue. As a charming part of that ceremony, which was performed by the Reverend Jenns, the Victoria Leiderkrantz serenaded the newly married couple from the veranda. The couple left for a honeymoon in Portland, Oregon.

As the twentieth century dawned, high-society weddings in Victoria continued to be more and more elaborate. It was a far cry from the days when weddings between HBC men and Native women took place in the custom of the country.

&#x204A;

Finally, the end of the journey, when the last rites were read over all those important pioneering spirits, also became something of a social extravaganza. From the very beginning, social status in the colony had dictated the way a person worshipped or the religion he chose and, at the end, Victoria funerals continued to reflect someone's allotted place in life.

Religious differentiation was connected with social standing, and one early observer in Victoria noted that

> we may assert that the religious sect was commonly determined by the extent of a man's business, or his position ... [It was] the Church of England, the "state church" as it was called by many, [that] contained the bankers, lawyers, wholesale dealers and the governing class.
>
> "Just as with their augmented resources the people erect comfortable houses," said a visitor, "so they seek to provide themselves with a church suited to their advanced social position."[127]

The first church on Vancouver Island was erected on twenty acres of land granted by the HBC to the Church of England. The Reverend Edward Cridge, who had replaced the Reverend Staines in 1855, became the minister of "Christ's Church," which later became the cathedral (1865) and was destroyed by fire in 1869. Naturally, this was to become the established church and, as such, would control status among the governing class.

The Governor and his family sat in the "Governor's Pew," a large square apartment with a table, cushioned seats, carpets, and hassocks. One's social standing was determined by the proximity of his pew to that of the Governor's, and people sought to court the Governor's favour by sitting in the free seats behind his pew. Seats were occupied in the gallery near the organ, and a few ladies and gentlemen sang in the choir. Hymns only were sung during the service. A great deal of equipment for the church, as well as a 25,000-pound endowment, was sent out from England by Miss Burdett Coutts, relieving the financial burden of the Church considerably, so that by the time Bishop Hills arrived early in 1860 to take charge of the diocese, a new church, Saint John's, was in the process of construction.[128]

By April 1860, St. John's (the "Iron Church") was about to be consecrated and, again, had a primarily upper-class congregation.

In time, a mixture of religious denominations became apparent in Victoria, partly as a result of different ethnic backgrounds. The first Victoria directory lists two Anglican churches, one Roman Catholic, one Congregational, one Wesleyan, and one Presbyterian Church, and one Jewish synagogue.

Whatever church the upper-class citizens joined, church life would make up a large part of their social activity. Being involved in church work was an especially respectable role for the ladies. Organizing teas, bazaars, and other charitable endeavours occupied an enormous part of their lives and, more importantly, enabled them to be seen as pillars of society.

The church having played so large a part in their lives, it was hardly surprising that the funerals of some of the early colonists were splendidly extravagant. The funerals of the rich were always solemn, sedate occasions, when the virtues of the departed were extolled in a grand and elaborate manner.

Victoria's original cemetery, which was at the southwest corner of Douglas and Johnson streets, was closed by 1860 because of numerous problems, not the least of which had been stray dogs digging up some of the graves.

Edgar Fawcett reports in his *Some Reminiscences of Old Victoria* that, as a young boy in 1859, he witnessed coffins and corpses being removed from their original location and re-interred in the Quadra Street Cemetery, now Pioneer Square.

Even this cemetery outgrew itself, and it was decided that a new cemetery should be found.

[A] place where our children and children's children, as they wander through the winding avenues of that "City of the Dead" . . . will call to remembrance the early dead, and contemplate upon the mighty past.[129]

By 1873, burials were no longer taking place at Pioneer Square, as the land for Ross Bay Cemetery had been acquired the year before.

One of the first burials in Victoria was that of Charles Ross (after whom Ross Bay is named). Ross was the man who had first taken command of Fort Victoria, but his leadership was brief, as he died a few months later and was buried in the old burying ground near the gully on Johnson Street. On the ninety-ninth anniversary of his death, in June 1943, a monument to him was unveiled and stands today in Pioneer Square, where his remains are now buried.

Ross Bay Cemetery soon became the very epitome of grandeur with its "winding avenues" and elegant memorials. Many important people were laid to rest there. By 1881, the cemetery had over a thousand graves, the most important situated near the circular carriageways, an indication that wealth demanded a more strategic, easily accessible location. The BC Funeral Furnishing Company (owned by the Hayward family) conducted many of those early funerals.

Hearses were elaborate black-and-silver contraptions, with a profusion of carvings and trimmings. The horses drawing the hearse were draped in black net, from which hung many tassels. A child's hearse, by contrast, was white and drawn by Shetland ponies draped in white net. They were all solemn affairs, conducted with pomp and ceremony and the appropriate degree of dignity.

By far the most impressive of all funerals was that of James Douglas. And, just as this narrative began with the Douglas family, so it should end with that solemn occasion in 1877, when the Father of British Columbia passed on. Victoria was plunged into deep mourning: buildings were draped in black, schools were closed, and only the rumble of navy guns in the distance broke the solemn silence as the funeral party wound its way to Ross Bay.

Earlier, Bishop Cridge had preached the sermon in the church that he and James Douglas had founded together, and declared that "the right man had been in the right place" at a time when BC had needed good leadership. The respect given him was rightly deserved and proves that indeed "no history of the province can be written without Sir James Douglas forming the central figure."[130]

# CHAPTER TWELVE

# And in Conclusion

"Above stairs" society in early Victoria was a composite of many things. The upper-class settlers were predominantly British, and it was they who turned the city into a natural breeding ground for anyone who might consider himself part of an old aristocracy in a new world. With money, power, and a natural inclination to dominate, these new aristocrats successfully managed to become the ruling hierarchy for the first seventy-five years of Victoria's existence.

The wind of change, however, was already blowing by the time war was declared in 1914, and with the changes would come a new order. An industrial revolution in Britain, women's rights, a declining economy in British Columbia, and a devastating world war had all contributed to the process that ultimately led to the destruction of that old way of life. Through the lives of some of the families who made up the early high society of Victoria, we have glimpsed those years.

It is easy to imagine the charm, the elegance, the beauty, and the leisurely pace of life that existed in Victoria's halcyon years, and it is still pleasant to reflect on that scenario from today's perspective. It was a time when upper-class ladies and gentlemen occupied themselves with pursuits that seemed to them to be of the greatest importance but would be deemed trivial in today's world.

The ladies of Victoria, for example, spent a great deal of their time keeping scrapbooks up to date. In these books they kept a variety of clippings—favourite poems, old photographs, pressed flowers of a sentimental nature, and sometimes even some cleverly worded sayings such as "No person wants STRAW spelled backward on the end of his nose."

One young Victoria lady's collection contains some "Hints on Selecting a Husband." This piece asserted that there are four significant types of head to be found in the male population. One type is weak, another is conceited and unreasonable, one is strong and combative, and one is strong and balanced. It was up to the young lady to be smart enough to choose the right head type when selecting her husband.

If that task proved too difficult, the article encouraged her to study the thumbs of her gentleman friend. They were considered to be a key. For instance, if the "thumb be long and well-shaped and the lower or nail joint is of nearly the same length as the upper joint, there is a good balance of will power and intellect."[131]

Young ladies of Victoria obviously used a great deal of energy thinking about their future husbands. One delightful clipping, titled "How to Cook a Husband," instructed them on how to behave once they had found their man.

As Mr. Glass said of the hare, you must first catch him. Having done so, the mode of cooking him, so as to make a good dish of him is as follows:— Many good husbands are spoiled in the cooking; some women go about it as if their husbands were bladders, and blow them up. Others keep them constantly in hot water, while others freeze them by conjugal coldness. Some smother them with hatred, contention and variance, and some keep them in pickle all their lives.

These women always serve them up with tongue sauce. Now it cannot be supposed that husbands will be tender and good if managed in that way. But they are, on the contrary, very delicious when managed as follows: Get a large jar called the jar of carefulness (which all good wives have on hand), place your husband in it and set him near the fire of conjugal love; let the fire be pretty hot, and especially let it be clear—above all, let the heat be constant. Cover him over with affection, kindness and subjection. Garnish with modest, becoming familiarity, and the spice of pleasantry; and if you had kisses and other confectioneries let them be accompanied with a sufficient portion of secrecy, mixed with prudence and moderation. We would advise all good wives to try this recipe and realize how admirable a dish a husband is when properly cooked.[132]

Another excellent maxim that the young ladies of Victoria might have believed can be found in the words "Be obstinately just, Indulge no passion, and Deceive no trust," clipped into one scrapbook.

Those same prim and proper women also enjoyed the risqué humour found in another clipping:

The lady was leaning on the arm of an elegant and wealthy young man and leading her little daughter by the hand, when suddenly the child cried: "Oh, ma, ma, look there! See that gentleman that's passing. Don't you know him?" "No-no, my child," the lady replies. 'Why, mamma, he was my pa last year." Ma faints![133]

Elizabeth Rithet was a prime example of a young woman in Victoria who kept an elaborate scrapbook. Katherine O'Reilly was equally indulgent in her collection of memorabilia and was also a prolific writer and journal keeper.

Another pastime that occupied the ladies for the greater part of every day was the selection of and changing into their outfits (sometimes as many as five times in one day) in order to suit the social function in which they were participating. They might appear at breakfast time in a riding habit in order to take an early morning ride, but other meals required a more suitable and appropriate dress. Even for the ritual of afternoon teas, it was appropriate to change into a tea gown. No sooner was tea over than it was time to change again and dress for dinner.

A particularly hypocritical aspect of Victorian life can be found in the general attitude toward the wearing of cosmetics. If a lady wanted to use them in those days, it had to be with such discretion that the final effect appeared to be nothing more than a mere improvement on nature. Only actresses or women of ill repute would openly admit to using any form of makeup. Chinese Leaves for the Cheeks and Lips, and such things as Magnetic Rock Dew Water of the Sahara or Venus's Toilet Water (lotions for the skin) were used sparingly. Most women had to be content with a vigorous application of soap and water or sponge and brush to a contrast of colour on an otherwise pale face.

Although cosmetic improvement had to be minimal, the dressing of hair was both elaborate and time-consuming. Ladies' maids often spent hours combing, brushing, plaiting, and even polishing their mistresses' hair, until the desired effect was created.

And while all these frivolities were taking place, the men went about their business, involving themselves in financial deals and aiming for political greatness. It was a time of new building, exciting discoveries, and new inventions, and a general transformation of Victoria, from tranquil hamlet to boom town, was taking place. As a result, men of initiative took part, grabbing at opportunities as they came along.

Dinner parties were scenes of important political decision-making, and many a glass of port and a cigar shared with a colleague in the smoking room would seal a business deal. The smoking room, incidentally, was the special room added to most upper-class houses, along the lines of the one first installed by Queen Victoria at Osborne House in order to accommodate, in her words, gentlemen who wished to indulge the disgusting habit of smoking.

Throughout the first seventy-five years of Victoria's growth, social divisions were always very apparent. These divisions were reflected in the way the settlers worshipped, the way they entertained themselves, their sporting activities, and where they sent their children to school. Class distinction was of the utmost importance, even to where and how residents were laid to rest at the end of their journey through life.

The population in those years fluctuated at an alarming rate. The initial influx of humanity as a result of the two gold rushes, almost twenty-five thousand people, encouraged both speculation and prosperity. But, as often happens, much of the initial prosperity disappeared once the population settled down to six thousand.

Following a somewhat depressed economy after the 1860s, Victoria's population took a dramatic plunge to around fifteen hundred and did not rise again until the early 1880s. The new aristocrats managed to weather every economic storm as it came along. For some, it even meant that their accumulated wealth grew to phenomenal proportions. Those who were wise invested in property, and their offspring were the beneficiaries for years. As one descendant of a well-to-do pioneer family noted in the 1980s, "Their wealth was handed down to us. We did not earn it. Today, we are merely the caretakers."[134]

After a real estate collapse in the early part of the twentieth century and the First World War, some of the original upper class lost vast fortunes. More important was the loss of the old familiar way of life. Future generations found themselves forced into a simpler lifestyle as they tried to rebuild those fortunes. Nothing, it would seem, was ever the same again in Victoria, and that intriguing time of upper- and lower-class society, when each knew his place and accepted his position in life, was gone.

Social event at the Alexandra Club, c. 1911.
IMAGE F-06593 COURTESY OF ROYAL BC MUSEUM, BC ARCHIVES

The leisurely, elegant lifestyle depicted in this text was available only to those who were financially secure and well placed in life. If this were the case, an exceptionally privileged existence could be enjoyed. For those settlers of means, or for those who later made their fortunes and managed to infiltrate the inner sanctum of high society, life in Victoria's early years was indeed pleasant and comfortable and, in many respects, very similar to the life being led in England by people in similar circumstances.

Nonetheless, in Victoria it was a unique time, a time when elegance and tradition mingled side by side with a new, raw, cosmopolitan environment, and there was "an impatience to grow very quickly into a position which had taken older cities decades to attain."[135]

Victoria's aristocrats who lived "above stairs" had helped to make it happen.

# FAMILY LINEAGES

## DOUGLAS FAMILY

James Douglas   m   Amelia Connolly
1803–1877               1812–1890

### 13 children

| | | |
|---|---|---|
| Amelia 1829–1830 | Ellen 1836–1837 | Rebecca 1849–1849 |
| Alexander 1831–1834 | Jane 1839–1909 | James 1851–1883 |
| John 1833–1833 | Agnes 1841–1928 | Martha 1854–1933 |
| Maria 1834–1835 | Alice 1844–1913 | |
| Cecilia 1834–1865 | Margaret 1846–1848 | |

## SKINNER FAMILY

Thomas Skinner   m   Mary Lowdham Goode
1812–1889                 1816–1896

### 9 children

| | | |
|---|---|---|
| Ambrose 1842–1880 | Ernest 1847–1918 | Constance 1853–1904 |
| Robert 1844–1909 | Annie 1849–1932 | Ada Jane 1856–1924 |
| Francis 1845–1851 | Mary 1851–1942 | Emily 1858–1907 |

## PEMBERTON FAMILY

Joseph Despard Pemberton   m   Teresa Jane Grautoff
1803–1877                                    1842–1916

### 6 children

| | |
|---|---|
| Frederick Bernard 1865–1947 | Ada Died 1958 |
| Joseph Jr. 1873–1916 | Sophia 1869–1959 |
| William Died 1877 | Harriet 1871–1949 |

## CREASE FAMILY

Henry Pering Pellew Crease   m   Sarah Lindley
1823–1905                                 1826–1922

### 8 children

| | |
|---|---|
| 1st son died in infancy | Josephine 1864–1947 |
| Mary Mabley 1854–1915 | Lindley 1867–1940 |
| Susan 1855–1947 | Henry 1869–1870 |
| Barbara 1857–1883 | Arthur 1872–1967 |

## O'REILLY FAMILY

Peter O'Reilly   m   Caroline Trutch
1828–1905          1831–1899

4 children

Frances Joseph   1866–1941          Mary Augusta   1869–1876
Charlotte Kathleen   1867–1945          Arthur John   1873–1946


## TRUTCH FAMILY

Joseph Trutch   m   Julia Hyde
1826–1904          1827–1895

No children

Trutch lineage has continued through Joseph's brother, John.


## RITHET FAMILY

Robert Paterson Rithet   m   Elizabeth Jane Munro
1844–1919                1853–1952

3 children

Gertude Alice   1877–1945          Edward Paterson   1881–1901
John Alexander   1878–1942


## BARNARD FAMILY

Francis Jones Barnard   m   Ellen Stillman
1838–1889                1839–1889

3 children

Frank Stillman   1856–1936          George Henry   1868–1954
Alice Mara   1858–1906

# ENDNOTES

### Introduction: In the Institutions of the Old
1. Pelly to Hawes, October 24, 1846, *Great Britain, Parliament, House of Commons, Sessional Papers, 1846–48*, No. 619, p. 5.
2. Akrigg, G.P.V. and Helen B. Akrigg, *British Columbia Chronicle—1847–71, Gold & Colonists*, pp. 21, 22.
3. Blakey Smith, Dorothy, ed., "A Reminiscence of 1850 (Appendix 2)," p. 81, in *The Reminiscences of John Sebastian Helmcken*.

### Chapter One: The Douglas Family
4. Tod, John, "History of New Caledonia and the Northwest Coast, Victoria, 1878," unpublished MS in BC Archives, cited in Pethick, Derek, *James Douglas: Servant of Two Empires*, p. 8.
5. Blakey Smith, Dorothy, ed., "A Reminiscence of 1850 (Appendix 2)," p. 281, in *The Reminiscences of John Sebastian Helmcken*.
6. Ibid.
7. Blakey Smith, Dorothy, ed., *The Reminiscences of John Sebastian Helmcken*, p. 120.
8. Ibid., p. 131.
9. Letters from Douglas to Martha Douglas, June 11, 1873, BC Archives.
10. Pethick, Derek. *Victoria: The Fort*, p. 228 (n. 96).
11. Douglas to Dallas, July 23, 1867, Sir James Douglas, Correspondence Outward, BC Archives.
12. Douglas to James Douglas, April 8, 1868, BC Archives.
13. Blakey Smith, Dorothy, ed., "In the Early Fifties (Appendix 2)," p. 293, in *The Reminiscences of John Sebastian Helmcken*.

### Chapter Two: The Skinner Family
14. Robinson, Leigh Burpee, *Place of Shoaling Water*, p. 69.
15. Ibid.
16. Anderson, James. "Notes and Comments on early days and events in British Columbia," BC Archives.

17. *Colonist*, August 1860.
18. *Colonist*, August 1861.
19. *Colonist*, May 1864.
20. *Colonist*, December 15, 1860.

### Chapter Three: The Pemberton Family
21. Pemberton, J. D., *Facts and Figures Relating to Vancouver Island and British Columbia*, p. 86.
22. Douglas to Barclay, January 16, 1852, BC Archives.
23. Barclay to Pemberton, July 28, 1854, BC Archives.
24. Memo from W. F. Tolmie to Thomas Fraser, Secretary of the Hudson's Bay Company, November 13, 1861, BC Archives.
25. Sampson, H. S., "My Father, Joseph Despard Pemberton: 1821–93" *BCHQ*, Vol. VIII, No. 2, p. 121.
26. *Colonist*, March 25, 1864.
27. Sampson, op. cit., p. 124.
28. Lugrin, N. de B., *The Pioneer Women of Vancouver Island*, p. 286.
29. Ibid.
30. Sampson, op. cit., p. 123.
31. Ibid, p. 125.

### Chapter Four: The Crease Family
32. *Colonist*, December 22, 1859.
33. *Government Gazette Extraordinary, March/May 1870*, "Debate on the subject of Confederation of Canada," cited in Pethick, Derek, *Summer of Promise*, p. 54.
34. Sarah Crease to H.P.P. Crease, July 1888, Crease Collection, BC Archives.
35. Crease, Susan Reynolds, *Reminiscences*, BC Archives.
36. Johnson-Dean, Christina B., "The Crease Family Archives," p. 12, BC Archives.
37. Ormsby, Margaret A., ed., *A Pioneer Gentlewoman in British Columbia: The Recollections of Susan Allison*, p. 17.
38. Ibid.
39. Johnson-Dean, op. cit., p. 13.
40. Ibid., p. 20.

[41] Ibid.

[42] Crease Collection, Letters from Sarah Crease, 1864, BC Archives.

[43] Aberdeen to Crease—Memorandum, City of Victoria Archives.

[44] *Colonist*, January 3, 1896.

**Chapter Five: The O'Reilly Family**

[45] "Some Irish Figures in Colonial Days," *BCHQ*, Vol. XIV, January to April, 1950, p. 69 (n. 31).

[46] *Colonist*, Letter to the Editor, May 1859.

[47] "Some Irish Figures in Colonial Days," op. cit., p. 73.

[48] O'Reilly Collection, Letters to Caroline Trutch, BC Archives.

[49] Ibid., Letters to Kathleen O'Reilly from Baroness Macdonald of Earnscliffe, BC Archives.

[50] *Colonist*, April 1885.

**Chapter Six: The Trutch Family**

[51] Trutch to Emily Pinder, April 29, 1850, Trutch Papers, Howay-Reid Collection, UBC Library.

[52] Lynch, Hollis R., "Sir Joseph William Trutch, a British-American Pioneer on the Pacific Coast," *Pacific Historical Review*, Vol. 30, August 1961, p. 249.

[53] Jackman, S.W., *The Men at Cary Castle*, p. 20.

[54] Ibid., p. 22.

[55] Ibid., p. 21.

[56] Ibid., p. 22.

[57] Ibid., p. 24.

[58] *Colonist*, July 1895.

[59] Fisher, Robin, "Joseph Trutch and Indian Land Policy," in *Historical Essays on British Columbia*, p. 257.

[60] Ibid.

[61] Ibid., p. 275.

**Chapter Seven: The Rithet Family**

[62] Ireland, W., "British Columbia's American Heritage," *Canadian Historical Association Annual Report for 1948*, p. 68.

[63] Rithet Letterbook, Rithet to Mrs. Sutton, April 16, 1870, BC Archives.

[64] Ibid., Rithet to A. Welch, August 24, 1871.

[65] Ibid., August 25, 1871.

[66] *Colonist*, November 1884.

[67] Private Rithet Collection, notebook dated June 6, 1906.

**Chapter Eight: The Barnard Family**

[68] *The British Columbian*, June 14, 1862.

[69] Kerr, *Biographical Dictionary of Well-known British Columbians*, Vol. III, p. 1068.

[70] Akrigg, G.P.V., and Helen B., *British Columbia Chronicle—1847–71, Gold & Colonists*, p. 315.

[71] *The British Columbian*, May 4, 1864.

[72] Jackman, S.W., *The Men at Cary Castle*, p. 106.

[73] *Victoria Times*, November 20, 1945.

[74] Ibid.

**Chapter Nine: Balls, Banquets, and Enlightened Entertainments**

[75] Walden, F.E., *Social History of Victoria*, pp. 35, 36.

[76] *Colonist*, August 1890.

[77] "The Diary of Robert Melrose," *BCHQ*, 7 (1943), p. 209.

[78] "The Diary of Martha Cheney Ella, 1853–56," J.K. Nesbitt ed., *BCHQ*, 13 (1949), p. 268.

[79] Journal of Lieutenant Wilson, R.E., August 2, 1858, BC Archives.

[80] Ibid., December 2, 1858, BC Archives.

[81] Macfie, Matthew, *Vancouver Island and British Columbia*, p. 79.

[82] Diary of Martha Douglas, 1867, p. 8, BC Archives.

[83] Victoria *Gazette*, November 13, 1858.

[84] Walden, F. E., *Social History of Victoria*, p. 112.

[85] Ibid., p. 114

[86] Ibid.

[87] Anderson, James R., "Notes and Comments on the early days and events of British Columbia," BC Archives, pp. 180, 181.

[88] Walden, F.E., *Social History of Victoria*, p. 132.

[89] *Colonist*, August 1886.

[90] Ibid., August 13, 1879.

[91] Ibid.

[92] Ibid., May 1866.

[93] Ibid.

[94] Ibid., August 30, 1890.

[95] Ibid.

[96] Ibid.

[97] Ibid., January 1899.

[98] O'Reilly Collection, BC Archives.

[99] Barnard Collection, BC Archives.

[100] *Times Colonist*, "Islander" section, January 1985, "The Windermere Building: Then and now—home of the Alexandra Club," by Elizabeth Gordon.

[101] *Colonist*, August 28, 1955, "Lucky for Arion Club—Group Sings Paean to No.13," by H.B. Binny (from Arion Club By-Laws).

[102] Ibid.

[103] *Victoria Home Journal*, 1890s.

**Chapter Ten: Costumes, Conveyances, and Conversations**

[104] Journal of Lieutenant Wilson, R.E., August 2, 1858, BC Archives.

[105] O'Reilly Collection, Correspondence from Kathleen O'Reilly to parents, January–April, 1897, BC Archives.

[106] Carr, Emily, *The Book of Small*, pp. 90, 91.

[107] Parker, R.V., *No Horsecars in Paradise*, p. 21.

[108] Baskerville, Peter A., *Beyond the Island—an Illustrated History of Victoria*, p. 66.

[109] Parker, R.V., op. cit., p. 22.

[110] *Times Colonist*, "Islander" section, May 10, 1992, "George helped the rich put on the dog," by Valerie Green.

[111] *Times Colonist*, "Islander" section, August 10, 1980, "Victoria's First Automobiles," by Derek Pethick.

[112] HMS *Trincomalee*, a sailing frigate.

**Chapter Eleven: Residences, Rituals, and Rites**

[113] Ireland, Willard E., "Captain Walter Colquhoun Grant," *BCHQ*, Vol. XVII, Nos. I and 2, p. 108.

[114] Cotton, Peter, *Vice Regal Mansions of British Columbia*, p. 17.

[115] Blakey Smith, Dorothy, ed., *The Reminiscences of John Sebastian Helmcken*, pp. 127, 128.

[116] Robinson, Leigh Burpee, *Esquimalt: Place of Shoaling Water*, pp. 68, 69.

[117] Crease Collection, Crease to Wright & Sanders, 27 April, 1872, BC Archives.

[118] *Times Colonist*, "Islander" section, October 13, 1981, "Joseph Trutch—the man and his home," by Elizabeth Gordon.

[119] *The Daily Colonist*, June 6, 1948, "Old Homes & Families," by J.K. Nesbitt.

[120] Ibid., November 18, 1951.

[121] *Colonist*, April 15–16, 1957.

[122] Hibbert, Christopher, *Daily Life in Victorian England*, p. 9.

[123] Blakey Smith, Dorothy ed., "A Reminiscence of 1850 (Appendix 2)," pp. 296, 297, in *The Reminiscences of John Sebastian Helmcken*.

[124] "The Diary of Martha Cheney Ella, 1853–1856," *BCHQ* 13 (1949).

[125] Crease Collection, Barbara Lindley to Mary Smith Crease, April 28, 1853, BC Archives.

[126] *The Daily Colonist*, April 3, 1949, "Old Homes & Families," by J.K. Nesbitt.

[127] Macfie, Matthew. *Vancouver Island and British Columbia*, p. 417, cited in F.E. Walden's *Social History of Victoria*, p. 120.

[128] Ibid., p. 122.

[129] Fawcett, Edgar, *Some Reminiscences of Old Victoria*, p. 89.

[130] *Victoria Colonist*, August 4, 1877.

**Chapter Twelve: And in Conclusion**

[131] Winter Collection, Album of Maggie Winter (née Johnson), City of Victoria Archives.

[132] Ibid.

[133] Ibid.

[134] Interview with Richard H. Todd, September 1988.

[135] Walden, F.E., *Social History of Victoria*, p. 135.

# BIBLIOGRAPHY

**Books**

Akrigg, G.P.V. and Helen B. *British Columbia Chronicle—1778–1846, Adventures by Sea & Land*, Discovery Press, 1975.

——. *British Columbia Chronicle—1847–1871, Gold & Colonists*, Discovery Press, 1977.

Baskerville, Peter A. *Beyond the Island—An Illustrated History of Victoria*, Windsor Publications Ltd., Burlington, Ontario, 1986.

Begg, Alexander. *History of British Columbia—from Its Earliest Discovery to Present Time*, Ryerson Archives Series, 1894.

Blakey Smith, Dorothy (ed.). *The Reminiscences of Doctor John Sebastian Helmcken*, University of British Columbia Press, Vancouver, 1975.

Carr, Emily. *Klee Wyck*, Irwin Publishing, Toronto, 1941.

——. *The Book of Small*, Irwin Publishing, Toronto, 1942.

——. *The House of All Sorts*, Irwin Publishing, Toronto, 1944.

Cotton, Peter. *Vice Regal Mansions of British Columbia*, Elgin Publications Ltd. (for the British Columbia Heritage Trust), Vancouver, 1981.

Dunae, Patrick A. *Gentlemen Emigrants: From the British Public Schools to the Canadian Frontier*, Douglas & McIntyre, Vancouver, 1981.

Fawcett, Edgar. *Some Reminiscences of Old Victoria*, William Briggs, Toronto, 1912.

Friesen, J. and H.K. Ralston, (eds.). *Historical Essays on British Columbia*, Gage Publishing Limited, Toronto, 1980.

Green, Valerie. *Excelsior! The Story of the Todd Family*, Orca Book Publishers, Victoria, 1990.

——. *No Ordinary People—Victoria's Mayors Since 1862*, Beach Holme Publishers, Victoria, 1992.

Gregson, Harry. *A History of Victoria (1842–1970)*, The Victoria Observer Publishing Co. Ltd., Victoria, 1970.

Hayman, John (ed.). *Robert Brown and the Vancouver Island Exploring Expedition*, University of British Columbia Press, Vancouver, 1989.

Hibbert, Christopher. *Daily Life in Victorian England*, American Heritage Publishing Co. Inc., New York, 1975.

Howay, F.W. and E.O.S. Scholefield. *British Columbia from the Earliest Times to the Present* (4 Vols.), Vancouver, 1914.

Jackman, S.W. *The Men at Cary Castle*, Morriss Printing Company Ltd., 1972.

Kerr, J.B. *Biographical Dictionary of Well-known British Columbians*, Kerr & Begg, Vancouver, 1890.

Lugrin, N. de B. *The Pioneer Women of Vancouver Island*, Victoria, The Women's Canadian Club of Victoria, 1928.

Macfie, Matthew. *Vancouver Island and British Columbia: Their History, Resources & Prospects*, Longman, Roberts & Green, London, 1865.

Mallandaine, Edward. *First Victoria Directory, Victoria, 1860, Directory for 1863*, Victoria, 1863.

Ormsby, Margaret A. (ed.). *A Pioneer Gentlewoman in British Columbia: The Recollections of Susan Allison*, University of British Columbia Press, Vancouver, 1976.

Parker, Douglas V. *No Horsecars in Paradise*, Whitecap Books Ltd., a Railfare Book, 1981.

Pemberton, J.D. *Facts and Figures Relating to Vancouver Island and British Columbia*, Longman Green, London, 1860.

Pethick, Derek. *Victoria: The Fort*, Mitchell Press, Vancouver, 1968.

——. *James Douglas: Servant of Two Empires*, Mitchell Press, Vancouver, 1969.

——. *Summer of Promise*, Sono Nis Press, Victoria, 1980.

Reimer Derek, ed. *A Victorian Tapestry*, Sound Heritage, Vol. VII, No. 3. Aural History

Program, Royal BC Museum, BC Archives, Victoria 1978.

Reksten, Terry. *The Dunsmuir Saga*, Douglas & McIntyre, Vancouver/Toronto, 1991.

Robinson, Leigh Burpee. *Esquimalt: Place of Shoaling Water*, Quality Press, Victoria, 1947.

*Victoria, B.C., Centennial Celebrations 1862–1962*, Flynn Bros. Publishing Ltd., Victoria, 1962 (reprinted 1987).

Waddington, A. *The Fraser Mines Vindicated*, Victoria, 1858.

**Articles and Archival Sources**

Anderson, James. "Notes and Comments on early days and events in British Columbia, Washington and Oregon, 1925," Royal BC Museum, BC Archives.

Ella, Martha. "The Diary of Martha Cheney Ella, 1853–1856," ed. J.K. Nesbitt, *BC Historical Quarterly*, Vol. 13 (1949).

Fisher, Robin. "Joseph Trutch and Indian Land Policy," in *Historical Essays on British Columbia*, cited in *B.C. Studies*, XII (1971–72).

Ireland, Willard E. "Captain Walter Colquhoun Grant—Vancouver Island's First Independent Settler," *BCHQ*, Vol. XVII (1953).

Johnson-Dean, Christina B. "The Crease Family Archives—a Record of Settlement and Service in British Columbia," Royal BC Museum, BC Archives, 1982.

Lamb, W. Kaye. "Some Notes on the Douglas Family," *BCHQ*, Vol. XVII (1953).

Lynch, Hollis R. "Sir Joseph William Trutch, a British-American Pioneer on the Pacific Coast," *Pacific Historical Review*, Vol. 30, August 1961.

Mara, John Andrew. Diary, Private family collection.

Melrose, R. "The Diary of Robert Melrose," *BCHQ*, Vol. 7 (1943).

Nesbitt, J.K. *Old Homes & Families*, Royal BC Museum, BC Archives.

Ormsby, M.A. "Some Irish Figures in Colonial Days," *BCHQ*, Vol. 14 (January–April, 1950).

Sampson, Harriet S. "My Father, Joseph Despard Pemberton: 1821–1893," *BCHQ*, Vol. 8 (1944).

Tod, John. "History of New Caledonia and the Northwest Coast," Victoria, 1878, Royal BC Museum, BC Archives.

Walden, F.E. *Social History of Victoria, 1858–1871*, B.A. Thesis, University of British Columbia, Vancouver, 1951.

Wilson, Lieutenant Charles, R.E. Journal, (1858) Royal BC Museum, BC Archives.

**Newspapers and Periodicals**

*British Columbia Historical Quarterly*
*The British Columbian*
*Daily Colonist*
*Times Colonist (Islander)*
*Victoria (British) Daily Colonist*
*Victoria Daily Times*
*The Victoria Journal*

**Archives**

City of Victoria Archives
Royal BC Museum, BC Archives
Saanich Archives
Special Collections and University Archives Division, University of British Columbia

# INDEX

Ah Chu, 66
Alexandra Club, 53, 65, 139–143
Alexandra Suspension Bridge, 63, 75, 87
Angela College, 65
Arion Club, 143, 173
Automobile Club, 167

Bachelors' Hall, 21, 121, 126
Bernhardt, Sarah, 77
Bowker, John Sylvester, 202
Butterick, Ebenezer, 149

Carr, Emily, 159, 201
Chinese culture, 66
Cridge, Reverend, 117, 128, 207
Crystal Palace, 45

*Delineator*, 150, 153
Driard Hotel, 70, 201
Dunsmuir, Jessie, 77, 146, 156

East India Company, 31
Empress Eugénie, 151, 155

Genge, Lawrence, 96, 103, 105, 157, 191, 206
Gibson, Charles Dana, 152
Goodrich, Lady, 141

Hart, Dr. Edward Charles, 163
Hudson's Bay Company, 2, 6, passim

Jockey Club, 131

Kent, Herbert, 133, 143

Lindley, Dr. John, 61

Macdonald, Sir John and Lady, 70, 76, 78
Mechanics' Institute, 130
Mouat, Captain W.A., 128
Mount Radford School, 59, 85, 88
Munro, Alexander, 100, 103, 105, 190

Pankhurst, Mrs., 142
Pearse, B.W., 55, 62, 127, 128
Philharmonic Society, 128
Puget Sound Agricultural Company, 11, 30, 125

residences, 176–199
Reverend Staines, 22, 36, 207
Royal Engineers, 63, 87, 123, 126

Scott, Robert, 75, 76
Ships
  *Amphion*, 77
  *Bacchant*, HMS, 160
  *Brother Jonathan*, 43
  *Cameleon*, 63
  *Columbia*, 10
  *Commodore*, 11
  CPR Empress ships, 101
  *Enterprise*, 112
  *Favourite*, 85
  *Fort Yale*, 110
  *Grappler*, 29, 37, 43
  *Harpooner*, 8
  *Lusitania*, 108, 116, 117
  *Matthew*, 18
  *Monarch*, HMS, 29, 33
  *Norman Morison*, 10, 30–32, 47
  *Princess Louise*, 133
  *Princess Royal*, 105
  *Satellite*, HMS, 33
  *Sparrowhawk*, HMS, 63, 83, 88
  *Tory*, 11, 125
Singer, Isaac, 149
Stanhope, Captain, 77

tea time, 199, 201
Tingley, Stephen, 111
Todd, Bert, 163, 164, 166, 167, 171

Union Club, 114, 142

*Victoria Home Journal*, 144, 154
Victoria, Queen, 26, 61, 76, 126, 154, 161, 184, 196, 199, 200, 214
*Vogue* magazine, 152, 153

Welch, Andrew, 98, 100, 101
Winter, George, 160–162, 174

# ACKNOWLEDGMENTS

I am delighted to be able to bring back to my readers this new, updated version of *Above Stairs*, which was first published in 1995. My initial thanks, therefore, go to my publisher, Ruth Linka, of TouchWood Editions, for her insight in enabling this to happen. I also wish to thank my meticulous and indomitable editor Marlyn Horsdal, who always manages to magically transform text into something far better.

This new edition can now stand proudly beside its companion book *Upstarts & Outcasts* (a "below stairs" look at life in early Victoria), published by TouchWood in 2000.

I would also like to reiterate my thanks to all those who gave generously of their time and knowledge in assisting me with the original writing of this book. Some of these kind people have passed away since 1995, but I feel they should be remembered and their names mentioned in this new edition. They were Mary Helmcken, Betty Beckett, Connie Nichols, Jessie Bellhouse, Trudi Skillings, Mary Mara, Bonita Jackson, and Sheila Anderson.

Additional thanks to the British Columbia Archives, the Victoria City Archives, and Caroline Duncan at the Saanich Archives for her assistance with new photographic material.

I would like to add my sincere thanks to Terry Stofer for assisting me during the production of this new edition by updating my computer knowledge (not an easy task—hey, I'm a writer not a techie!) and to all my "Table 44" friends (you know who you are) for always supporting me in all my writing endeavours. And especially to Joan Neudecker—I have enjoyed all our commiserations over writing projects through the years and much appreciate your encouragement and inspiration.

Last, but by no means least, my love and thanks to my family—especially David, who *still* doesn't understand why on earth writers need to keep on writing, but loves one anyway.

Valerie Green was born and educated in England and has a background in journalism, English literature and history. She has lived in Victoria, British Columbia, since 1968, where she works as a freelance writer. She is the former author of the *Saanich News* column "Pages from the Past," and her new monthly column "Conversations from the Past" is featured in the *Seaside Times*. Valerie is the author of many historical books set in the Pacific Northwest, including family biographies and mystery-suspense fiction.